The Story of
WINCKLEY SQUARE
PRESTON

Marian Roberts

The Story of
WINCKLEY SQUARE
PRESTON

Marian Roberts

Editor: Andrew Mather

Copyright © Marian Roberts 1988
Copyright © Preston Historical Society 2009

Cover: aerial photograph of Winckley Square courtesy of the *Lancashire Evening Post*
Marian Roberts in 2006 on page xii: courtesy of Linda Barton, Archivist to Preston Historical Society

This revised, second edition with additional text by
Alan Crosby and Aidan Turner-Bishop
published in 2009
by Preston Historical Society
20 Round Wood
Penwortham Preston PR1 OBN

www.prestonhistoricalsociety.org.uk

ISBN 978-0-9561098-0-4 Paperback
ISBN 978-0-9561098-1-1 Hardback

A CIP catalogue record for this book is available from the British Library

Design and production by Andrew Mather. Colour photography by Anthony Price
Printed and bound by H. Charlesworth & Co. Ltd, Wakefield

DEDICATION — FIRST EDITION

This little book has its origin in a talk about Winckley Square which I have given to many local associations.

In December 1980, my husband, Louis Dickinson Roberts, died of cancer. He suffered greatly, and in spite of the wonderful help and support of our district nurses it was a harrowing experience for both of us, patient and nurse.

I so much admire the work done at St Catherine's, which in 1980 was not yet a reality, that I have looked for a way of helping, and whenever I have been offered a fee for my talk I have asked, instead, for a donation to St Catherine's Hospice. These have been many and generous and now, it is hoped, the proceeds of the book will also help.

In its pages you will read of Sir Charles Brown, a Preston doctor, born in Winckley Square, who was on the staff of Preston Royal Infirmary from 1870 until 1922. He often wrote books of local interest, his own life story among them, the proceeds of which were in aid of Preston Royal Infirmary, which in those days received no State aid and was entirely dependent on voluntary contributions. It is his example I am following now in aid of St Catherine's Hospice.

In this book all the modern photographs of buildings in Winckley Square and some of the portraits have been generously provided by Mr Tony Damsell of Images Studio and Gallery in memory of his parents, Arthur and Mary Damsell, both of whom died of cancer.

Please help St Catherine's Hospice to continue its wonderful work by buying this book.

Marian Roberts

DEDICATED TO THE MEMORY OF MARIAN ROBERTS

The first edition of *The Story of Winckley Square, Preston* by Marian Roberts was published in 1988. She dedicated it to her late husband, Louis, with the proceeds of the book sales being donated to St Catherine's Hospice. This book, the second edition, is dedicated to Marian and likewise the proceeds of the sales of the book will be for the benefit of the same hospice.

I knew Marian for at least twenty years; she was put in touch with me by the celebrated local historian, Nellie Carbis from Grimsargh. I had known Nellie for some twenty years before this. Both these friendships grew from an interest in local history. Marian was initially seeking information about my great great grandfather, William Cross (1771–1827). My knowledge was rather scanty, but I did have a very nice miniature portrait of William and sent it to her. She subsequently told me that she was so overcome at seeing the subject of so much of her research that she burst into tears. Marian greatly admired William and always referred to him as 'My William'. He was the founder of Winckley Square, if that is the correct term, in the 1790s.

Marian was absolutely meticulous in her research of local history; no stone was left unturned and everything she wrote in her book will, without doubt, be correct. Her interest went far beyond Winckley Square to many projects in Preston and the surrounding district. She knew a great deal about leading figures in the town (now city) from past times.

The Guild of 1992 was a peak year for Marian and she was very active during the once in every twenty-years festivities. One of the highlights which gave her great joy was attending the Guild in August 1992 as my proxy, the Cross family having been Guild Burgesses since 1702.

Although I was able to provide Marian with some information of use to her, it was but a fraction of that which she provided for me as regards my family's history and connections with Preston. I would have known little about which without her help, including details of the founding of the Royal Cross School for the Deaf in the nineteenth century, now in a new location under a new name. Marian's research on my behalf went from before the Industrial Revolution, through the Cotton Famine of the 1860s that so devastated north-west towns then, and well into the twentieth century.

My memories of Marian could go on for a long time, but since she was a person for facts and being concise, it would be timely for the reader to move forward to enjoy and learn from this second edition of *The Story of Winckley Square, Preston.*

Anthony A. Cross
Tiverton, Devon
November 2008

CONTENTS

ACKNOWLEDGEMENTS *First edition*

I acknowledge with gratitude the assistance of:

Miss Vivienne Bennett, Museum and Art Officer of the Harris Museum & Art Gallery for permission to study the Addison Papers, and to reproduce plates numbered 11, 13, 14, 15, 16, 17, 18, 20, 22, 25, 28, 30, 31, 32, 33 and 37.

Mr Terry Shaw and Miss Ann Dennison of the Harris Reference Library for so readily making available an endless supply of books, newspapers, poll books, maps, census records, local history newspaper cuttings and for permission to make the necessary photocopies.

The department of the Preston Borough Solicitor for access to documents of historical importance in connection with Winckley Square.

The Estates Division of the Norwich Union Insurance Group, Surrey Street, Norwich, for information concerning number 6 Winckley Square.

Mrs W. J. M. Chaplin of Finsthwaite who deposited the document 'Draft Agreement on the Regulation of Winckley Square' in the Lancashire Record Office. Ref. DDPd 11/60.

Messrs Latham & Kirkham, Architects and Surveyors, 4 Regent Street, Preston, for permission to cite the example of the conditions imposed by Ellen Cross.

Mrs Phoebe Hesketh for permission to reproduce material from her book *My Aunt Edith* and to include her poem *The Ghost of Ribblesdale Place*.

Mr J. B. Hide and the Committee of Management of the Winckley Club for permission to quote from the documents of the Winckley Club, Preston.

The Editor of the *Lancashire Evening Post* for permission to use an article concerning Mr James Todd which appeared in that newspaper.

Mr Leo Warren of Newman College for information concerning all Catholic matters.

Mr Tony Damsell for photographs by Images Studio & Gallery and Mr Stephen Sartin who, at the eleventh hour, gave such practical help and support.

Our thanks to Bernard Dickinson Ltd of Tarleton and Fulwood for their help in funding this reprint.

Marian Roberts
1988

ACKNOWLEDGEMENTS *Second edition*

The publication of this second edition of Marian's book has only been made possible by the generosity of individual and corporate sponsors listed on the following page. On behalf of Preston Historical Society I thank them all wholeheartedly.

In 2006 when I first considered republishing this book I was reluctant, not being a historian, to undertake the required research. Fortunately, the gap in my historical knowledge was most ably filled by Alan Crosby, who has written the introduction, and Aidan Turner-Bishop, whose appreciation of Marian encapsulates what we all felt about her and still feel about her memory. Just before she died in 2007, Marian gave her approval to the venture. It is with real appreciation that I thank them both for their contributions, advice and encouragement.

I would also like to put on record my thanks to Anthony Cross, a direct descendant of William Cross, effectively the progenitor of Winckley Square, for writing the dedication to this edition.

My thanks also to the following: Emma Heslewood, Keeper of History at the Harris Museum & Art Gallery, for supplying digital images; Dorothy Walmsley for her meticulous proofreading; David Halewood for his book-selling advice; Linda Barton for her photograph of Marian; the Lancashire Record Office for assistance with maps; the *Lancashire Evening Post* for the use of their aerial photograph of Winckley Square; Anthony Price for the colour photography; Stephen Sartin for wise words; Robin Utracik for designing the Preston Historical Society emblem especially for this publication; Simon Mather of AMA DataSet Ltd; Nicola Mather for administrative assistance; John Bretherton of Cranden Press; and last, but not least, all the subscribers, who are listed at the back of the book.

It would be remiss of me not to mention all the staff of St Catherine's Hospice and to acknowledge the love and care which they provide for their patients. I hope the funds raised by the sale of *The Story of Winckley Square, Preston* will help them in their very special work.

Andrew Mather
President
Preston Historical Society
January 2009

SPONSORS

The Preston Historical Society is indebted to the following
for their generosity in funding the production
of this new edition of *The Story of Winckley Square, Preston.*

Donald and Dorothy Bamber
Diana Clarke
Lady Grenfell-Baines
Andrew and Julia Mather
Margaret Rose
Stephen Sartin
Joyce Sherrington
Aidan Turner-Bishop

AMA DataSet Limited
George Banks Ltd
Blackthorn Homes
E H Booth & Co Ltd
Champion Business Advisers Ltd
Freeman Rich
Friends of Lancashire Archives
Halewood & Sons
Hellewells (Preston) Ltd
James Todd & Co
Kings Abbot Rest Home
Moore & Smalley
Napthens Solicitors
St Wilfrid's RC Church
Winckley's
The Winckley Club

LIST OF ILLUSTRATIONS

Marian Roberts in 2006

Photograph by Linda Barton, Archivist to Preston Historical Society

MARIAN ROBERTS, an appreciation

Aidan Turner-Bishop

Marian Roberts, the author of *The Story of Winckley Square, Preston*, was one of the city's leading local historians in the late twentieth century.

She was born in the now demolished Bloomfield Street – opposite Emmanuel church, off Brook Street – in 1920. Her maiden name was Marian Weaver. With her family she moved, aged five, to Castle Chambers, home of the Refuge Assurance Company, opposite the Harris Museum. Her mother was the caretaker for 'the Refuge' and the family lived in a flat in the building. Marian remembered seeing from the window all the important events in the Flag Market. She left school at 14 and worked as a clerk in industry and with Lancashire County Council. Before she married, Marian was in repertory theatre and she toured the country with the Manchester Repertory Company. She lived in Castle Chambers until 1949 when she married Louis Roberts, whom she met in County Hall where they both worked. After living in Cottam, Broughton and Catforth, the couple eventually moved to Watling Street Road, Fulwood. When her beloved Louis died of cancer in 1980 – the same year in which Marian retired as a part-time ward secretary at the Royal Infirmary – she was naturally very bereft. To 'counter the unbearable depression', as she later said, she joined a class on palaeography at the Lancashire Record Office. 'It was just something to do at first, take my mind off things', she told reporter Elaine Singleton, 'It was a sort of therapy.' But from this there blossomed a passionate interest in and enthusiasm for Preston's local history that led, in 2004, to her receiving the British Association for Local History's Award for Personal Achievement. The *Lancashire Evening Post* described her, in 2002, as 'the uncrowned queen of this Lancashire city'.

As a local historian she combined her remarkable skill as an assiduous researcher – especially of Winckley Square and its families – and a tireless and joyful enthusiasm to communicate her discoveries and profound knowledge of the city's local history. At the time of her award Alan Crosby wrote in the British Association for Local History *Local History News*, that Marian, 'became an immensely popular speaker and lecturer to local societies of all sorts, talking about Winckley Square and her passion for local history and the way it brings the past of a town to life. She was a pillar of the Friends of the Harris Museum and the Preston Historical Society; an enthusiastic supporter of the Lancashire Record Office (through her good offices an important solicitors' collection was deposited there in 2002) and of Alston Hall, the nearby adult education college, whose history she also published.' Every penny of the royalties for her history of Winckley Square – first published in 1988 – and all her fees received for talks were donated to St Catherine's Hospice. She helped to raise many thousands of pounds for this cause from her local history work.

In 2001, aged 82 – a 'sprightly octogenarian' according to the local paper – she and her sister Elsie moved to Wymondham in Norfolk, to be close to her niece. Before she left Preston, she was celebrated with a civic reception at the Harris Museum, attended by her many admirers and those for whom she was 'something very special'. The move to Norfolk was a great wrench but Marian's enthusiasm for local history was undimmed. She soon began researching Wymondham's history, and remained in virtual touch with Preston's local historians by correspondence and the Winckley Square website.

Sadly, Elsie died in April 2006 and Marian passed away just ten months later in February 2007. For her, Preston was not just home but the greatest of towns, and now many of her carefully arranged and indexed papers on the history of Preston and its people are deposited in the University of Central Lancashire Library's Special Collections. But Marian herself was part of Preston's life and its history. All those who knew her felt she was somebody special. They were touched by her enthusiasm and passion and her great skills as a local historian. Above all, though, it was her kindness, generosity and goodness that impressed us, for Marian was simply a lovely, and much-loved, person.

THE HISTORICAL BACKGROUND
TO WINCKLEY SQUARE

Alan Crosby

In words which are often quoted, Daniel Defoe, writing in the early 1720s, summed up the character of Preston. This, he said, was 'a fine town, and tolerably full of people, but not like Liverpoole or Manchester [because] we come now beyond the trading part of the county. Here's no manufacture; the town is full of attorneys, proctors, and notaries . . . here is a great deal of good company.'[1] Defoe was a very perceptive observer, and he put his finger on the essential difference between Preston and other Lancashire towns in the reign of George I. This was not a manufacturing town, or a place which thrived on the hectic activity of international trade. Instead it was dominated by the professional classes, who had made it their own because for centuries Preston had been the county town. It was the administrative heart of both the County Palatine of Lancaster and the estates and business of the Duchy of Lancaster.[2] He might have added that Preston was also a flourishing market centre, much the most important in the county apart from Manchester, and was therefore also the retailing and social focus for a vast tract of north-west England.

These distinctive characteristics help to explain why Preston, in contrast to Manchester, Liverpool, and eventually Lancaster, did not develop any significant 'Georgian quarter'. The absence of rich merchants, with their national and international trading networks, and the lack of a new upwardly mobile class of entrepreneurs, meant that for much of the eighteenth century there was no great pressure to create exclusive and fashionable residential areas, segregated from the older, more workaday parts of the town. While Lancaster's merchants and shipowners, drawing their wealth from the West Indian and American trade, moved to grand new houses on the quay or in Dalton Square, in Preston the more traditional professional classes were content to live in their houses along Fishergate, Churchgate [now Church Street] and Friargate, and the town's leading retailers still lived, literally, above the shop.[3]

Nonetheless, change did come to the town in the final years of the eighteenth century, change which was of fundamental significance and, at that point, somewhat belatedly, the social segregation of rich from poor did at last emerge here as well. The leaders of town society – the older-established professional dynasties and those who drew new wealth from industry – increasingly chose to live in new and fashionable houses away from the bustle and increasing noise and dirt of the old town. It was that wish to escape from the growing unpleasantness of busy town life which was responsible for the development of Winckley Square and the high-status streets of the adjacent parts of Avenham. This process, which did not take place until the first decades of the nineteenth century – the period known generally as the Regency – created a classic townscape, with large and architecturally impressive houses set along leafy streets and around an elegant square. Preston's jewel may have been late in coming, but when it did it was of the finest quality, giving future generations one of the most attractive urban squares in the north of England. Although more recent generations have not always appreciated this legacy, and the town council has allowed changes which should never have been permitted, Winckley Square remains to delight us.

The population of Preston in the middle of the eighteenth century is hard to calculate, because there was no national census until 1801. The most reliable estimates suggest that there were perhaps 6,000 people in the early 1750s, and the first census figure for 1801 gives a population of just under 12,000, suggesting that numbers had doubled in about fifty years. Crucially, though, the expansion of the built-up area had not kept pace with that growth. Preston had physically grown outwards only a little over that time so, as the late Nigel Morgan so lucidly and searingly exposed in his work on Preston's housing, the result was a rapid increase in overcrowding and rapid deterioration of housing and sanitary conditions for the bulk of the townspeople.[4] The majority of the expansion took place after 1780 as the town began to industrialise. After 1801 growth was exceptionally fast, with 25,000 people in 1821 and over 51,000 by 1841. This is the background to the development of Winckley Square, for as urban problems multiplied, it became commensurately less desirable to live in the old town. Those who could do so began to move out into healthier, cleaner, quieter and more attractive areas.

Preston would undoubtedly have grown whatever the circumstances, but the exceptionally rapid expansion after 1780 was largely the result of the arrival of the cotton industry. John Horrocks, the greatest of the early 'cotton men', came to the town in 1791, by which time there were already several mills, but during the next fifteen years – largely under Horrocks's initiative – the industry grew at a remarkable rate. With its voracious appetite for labour it drew people from all points of the compass and within a decade had turned Preston into an industrial centre. The eastern side of the town, at the far end of Church Street and in what was soon christened New Preston (the New Hall Lane and Ribbleton Lane area), became a teeming, dirty working-class district, characterised by an ever-growing number of great mills, surrounded by terraced streets of distressingly poor housing, and with gross air pollution, inadequate water supplies, alarmingly bad sanitation, and a deplorable public health record. A second industrial zone emerged, from the 1780s onwards, on the north side of the town, around Fylde Road and the far end of Friargate where some of the earliest mills were located and where, from the mid-1790s, the canal basin provided a new focus for commercial and industrial activity. By 1810 Preston was one of the world's major cotton textile centres, a position it retained until the 1930s. By the 1850s it was arguably the unhealthiest major town in England, and as late as the 1870s it had the highest infant and child mortality rates in the country.[5]

Industry thus brought change on a dramatic scale. Every aspect of Preston life was altered for ever, from its physical environment and visual appearance, through its economic structure, to its social composition. The charming and gracious country town, noted by observers in the early and mid-eighteenth century as a place to which society resorted for the season, had enjoyed a delightful setting above the river, with the long line of the fells as a perfect backdrop. That pleasant environment swiftly gave way to all the negatives of the typical industrial centre – sufficient for Charles Dickens, in the early 1850s, to use Preston as one of the models for 'Coketown', the filthy and degraded setting of his novel *Hard Times*. But of course industry also brought wealth for those in the position to exploit its potential. Cotton was for some the source of undreamed of riches, even if for most it represented unremitting toil for small returns. Some groups benefited directly – the industrialists themselves, who owned the mills; the mushrooming middle classes who worked as managers and senior administrators in the industry; and the people who ran ancillary trades, supplying machinery and equipment, building contracts and transport services. Others benefited indirectly. The creation of an entirely new industrial sector was supported by an army of smaller clerks and a new lower middle-class of white collar workers. The shopkeepers and tradesmen of the town reaped the rewards of population growth and a flood of new business, and the professional classes – the lawyers, accountants, doctors and teachers – derived a lucrative additional trade from selling their services to the new industrial elite. Thus, leading shopkeepers, solicitors and medical men themselves became increasingly wealthy, and the social structure of the town was rapidly and permanently reshaped. All these groups had in common an increasing preference for suburban or separate living, and all sought, as soon as they could, to move away from the town centre.

The wealthiest groups pioneered the trend, for they had the greatest resources to develop new housing areas. To live above the shop was no longer socially acceptable, while to live in a main street was no longer pleasant – indeed, it was positively disagreeable. By 1800 there was tremendous pressure to move elsewhere, to socially superior enclaves well away from the poor and the pollution. The east end of town was simply impossible, because of its industry and filth, and the northern edge was similarly unpleasant (though later, as Fulwood grew, an address in the *far* north was particularly desirable). Moving westwards was more attractive, for the steep slope of Fishergate Hill was well away from industry and, until the railway came in 1840, it was quiet and clean. The road was not too busy, for only the narrow bridge at Broadgate as yet crossed the Ribble, and there were good views across the fields to the river and the marshes. But the south side of the town centre was best of all, for here there was a high bluff, overlooking the broad expanse of meadows and woods with the lovely hills in the distance. The landscape was unsullied by smoke and dirt, for industry was well away to the east, and there was no through road to generate noisy traffic.

The surroundings were agreeable, with the little stream known as the Syke flowing through a shallow valley running parallel with Fishergate. In the 1690s Preston Corporation had laid out gravelled walks at the southern end of this area, to provide a genteel and exclusive public amenity – it was one of the first provincial towns anywhere in England to undertake such formal landscaping – and ever since then Avenham had the reputation of being a 'respectable' district, known for its tranquil views.[6] Now it came into its own, and in the first years of the nineteenth century the land between Fishergate and the top of the slope above the river was gradually developed as a self-contained and highly desirable residential quarter. The Syke had become an open sewer, because it took most of the effluent from the south side of the town, but once it was culverted over in the 1820s and gurgled away out of sight and out of mind the development of Winckley Square, laid out across its subterranean course, could really get under way.

There was another special advantage to this location. Although Winckley Square was quiet, self-contained, and very superior, it was in fact only a hundred yards or so from another world, the lively bustle of Fishergate, and therefore the new residents could combine all the desirable qualities of an exclusive residential area with the convenience of being within walking distance of the centre. Only the super-rich, such as John Horrocks and his brother Samuel, moved right out of town – to Penwortham Hall and Lark Hill, respectively – and most of the elite were, for the first few decades, more than happy with Winckley Square. Read on, for now Marian Roberts tells their fascinating story.

[1] Daniel Defoe, *A Tour Through the Whole Island of Great Britain* (first published 1726; Penguin edition 1971) p. 548.

[2] It is interesting to note that this role remains crucial to the town's well-being, for the decline of cotton means that the County Council is now once again the largest employer, vying for that title with the University of Central Lancashire.

[3] For an overview of Lancashire's towns in the eighteenth and early nineteenth centuries, see Alan G. Crosby, 'Townscapes and Cityscapes', chapter 8 in Angus J. L. Winchester and Alan G. Crosby, *England's Landscape: The North West* (English Heritage/Collins, 2006).

[4] Nigel Morgan, *Vanished dwellings: early industrial housing in a Lancashire cotton town – Preston* (Mullion Books, 1990).

[5] For a general discussion of Preston in the Industrial Revolution see David Hunt, *A History of Preston* (Carnegie Publishing with Preston Borough Council, 1992) chapters 10 and 11.

[6] The particular importance of Preston, and the Avenham Walks, in the history of English urban design, is discussed in Peter Borsay, *The English Urban Renaissance: Culture and Society in the Provincial Town, 1660–1770* (Clarendon Press, 1989) esp. pp. 162–163. This book, which revolutionised our understanding of provincial towns in the seventeenth and eighteenth centuries, drew heavily upon Preston for its inspiration.

INTRODUCTION

Towards the end of the eighteenth century, Mr William Cross, attorney and Deputy Prothonotary for the County of Lancaster, returned from completing his legal studies in London, and, inspired by the squares in that city, decided on a similar project of his own. To that end he purchased a considerable amount of land. From a fellow-attorney, Mr Thomas Winckley, he purchased Town End Field, and much of Winckley Square occupies that land.

Reproduced below is Lang's Map of Preston in 1774, on which Town End Field can be seen lying on the southern side of Fishergate. St Wilfrid's Church, which pre-dates the Square, also stands on part of Town End Field. A stream, the Syke, ran across it from east to west, and as late as the end of the eighteenth century, snipe could be seen flying along its banks. In fact, the Fathers of St Wilfrid's Chapel were rebuked for shooting them!

In 1799 Mr Cross erected the first house in Winckley Square for his own occupation. It still stands, at the south-eastern corner of Winckley Street, and is now part of Tuson College [now Blackthorn Homes]. The entrance is in Winckley Street, and for a long time it was numbered 7 Winckley Street.

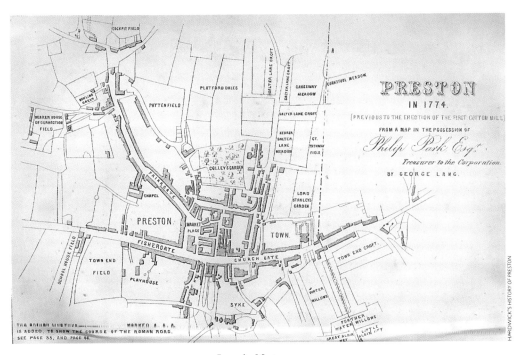

Lang's Map 1774

7 Winckley Street [now Blackthorn Homes]

The Grimshaw residence [now Inghams Solicitors]

1 Winckley Place and 1 Chapel Street

The second house to be built stands directly opposite, on the south-western corner of Winckley Street. It, too, had a door in that street, but its main entrance fronts the Square. This was built for Col Nicholas Grimshaw, who was seven times the Mayor of Preston, including twice as the Guild Mayor.

Building continued along this northern part of Winckley Square, though it was called Winckley Place at first, but the houses were built at the Chapel Street end. No. 1 Winckley Place was built by Mr Joseph Seaton Aspden, about 1801, and adjoining that, but with the front door in Chapel Street, was the next house, built by his friend, Mr Edward Gorst. Numbered 1 Chapel Street, this house long remained in the Gorst family.

The next house, built by Mr John Gorst, the younger brother of Mr Edward Gorst, was on the eastern, or left-hand side of the Square. It is the one occupied by the Norwich Union Insurance Company [now dwf Solicitors].

Hewitson tells us that 'About the time Mr John Gorst's house was erected, Mr Dalton of Thurnham Hall, who then lived at Avenham House, Preston, built the large square house for his town residence, where he dwelt many years.' This was erected

6 Winckley Square [now dwf Solicitors]

some distance from and south of Mr John Gorst's house. In the 1960s the house was demolished and in its stead we now have the Tax Office [now HM Revenue and Customs], Charles House, which is the most unfortunate modern intrusion into the Square.

There is, in the Lancashire Record Office, a draft agreement on the regulation of Winckley Square (Ref. DDPd 11/60). It is dated 1807 and says: 'Whereas the Sd several Persons Parties to these Presents are seized of or entitled to Houses or Lots for building Houses upon in a Square in Preston called or to be called Winckley Square . . . And whereas the Sd Wm Cross being greatly interested in promoting the building of good Houses and laying out the Sd oblong Piece of Land for the Convenience and Comfort of the Inhabitants of the Sd Square . . . hath agreed to permit the Sd Piece of Land to lie forever open and unbuilt upon. . . . And the Sd other Parties to these Presents have agreed to join with the Sd Wm Cross his heirs and Ass[igns] in the Expense of laying out the Sd oblong piece of Land as Pleasure Ground and of forever hereafter keeping the same in neat order . . . The Houses in the Square to be built three Stories high and to be uniform in front as near as may be so as to correspond in general appearance with the houses built by the Sd John Gorst and John Dalton and not to be of less annual value than forty pounds.'

Charles House, the Tax Office [now HM Revenue and Customs]

There were to be no factories, steam engines, disagreeable work or undertaking – nor any warehouses, necessary houses, midden steads – no shop, tavern, inn or house of public entertainment. The interior of the said oblong piece of land was to be laid out as pleasure ground, and the residents were to have keys to the general entrance gates.

Lastly, the proprietors were to meet every 15th April and 15th November at Mr Cross's office when a majority should have power to regulate the planting, lighting and cleansing of the Square.

For the greater part of the eigthteenth century, Preston had been an agricultural town and also the legal centre for the County of Lancaster; a town of broad streets and fine houses, as reported by Celia Fiennes and Daniel Defoe. But when, in 1791, Mr John Horrocks came to Preston, all that changed. In thirteen years he created, more or less single-handed, a cotton industry in Preston. By the year 1804 he was dead, aged only thirty-six, but the cotton industry grew and grew, and not very far away from Winckley Square were the crowded courts where the workers lived in squalor; where midden steads and open cess-pools were the order of the day. So it was not surprising that, in 1807, Mr Cross should note the general trend and be determined to keep Winckley Square a place apart.

By 1824, when a map was produced for Baines' *Lancashire*, the central area of Winckley Square does appear to have been 'laid out as pleasure-ground', and on the eastern side, immediately to the south of Mr Dalton's residence a new house apppeared. It was built by Mr Joseph Seaton Aspden, who had already built no. 1 Winckley Square. After living in that house for a while, he sold it to Mr Henry Fielding of Catterall, and then lived at this house, later numbered 9 Winckley Square, for the rest of his life. Notice Avenham House to the south and east of the Square, which was formerly the home of Mr John Dalton.

In 1827, Mr William Cross died suddenly, and it was not until 1830–31 that the next house was erected on the eastern side of the Square. This was on a plot of land adjoining the house of Mr John Gorst, on the southern side thereof; a plot originally purchased by another Gorst brother, Septimus. For some reason he never lived there, and the house erected in 1830–31 was built for the Rev Roger Carus Wilson, Vicar of Preston. This is the house currently occupied by Messrs Garratt Son & Flowerdew [now Napthens Solicitors].

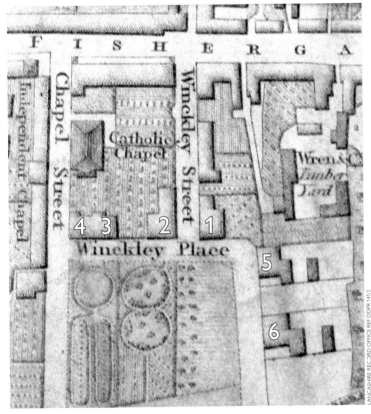

On the northern side of Winckley Place

1. William Cross
2. Nicholas Grimshaw
3. Joseph Seaton Aspden
4. Edward Gorst

On the eastern side of Winckley Place

5. John Gorst
6. John Dalton

LANCASHIRE RECORD OFFICE REF DDPR 141/2

Part of Shakeshaft's Map 1809 indicating the order in which the first houses were built

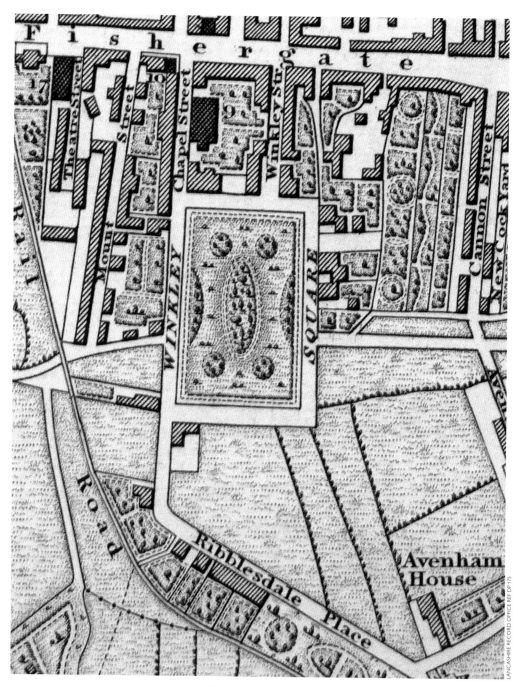

Baines' Map 1824

7 Winckley Square [now Napthens Solicitors]

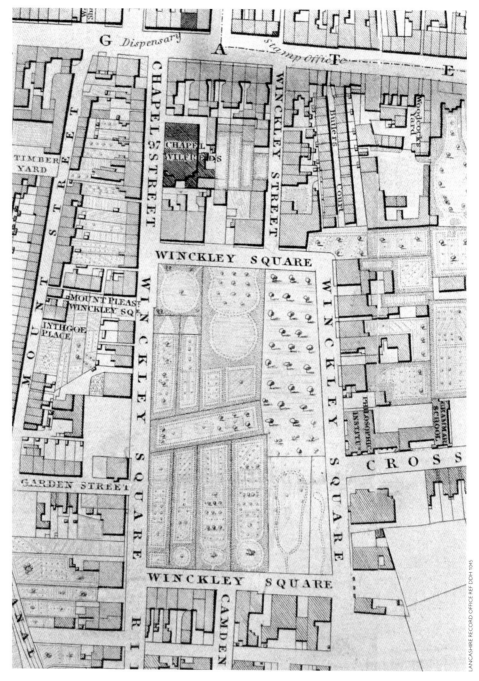

Myres' Map 1836

This can be seen on Myres' Map of 1836 and, in the central area, individual garden plots have taken place. The southern side of the Square, including part of Camden Place has been considerably developed.

WILLIAM CROSS

We now consider some of the early residents of these houses, all of whom were members of the legal profession and close friends. Thus we return to Mr William Cross, 'architect' of the project and first resident. He was the son of 'Honest' John Cross, attorney and Deputy Prothonotary for the Court of Common Pleas at Lancaster. Father and son lived in a house in Fishergate, William's mother having died shortly after his birth in 1771. In 1799, the year in which work commenced on the house in Winckley Street, John Cross died and William moved into the completed house with his maternal aunt, Mary Assheton, one of the Asshetons of Downham Hall, for it was she who had brought up the infant William Cross when his mother died.

William Cross, portrait by unknown artist

On his father's death William Cross was appointed Deputy Prothonotary in his stead; the office adjoined his house in Winckley Street.

In 1797, because of the threat of invasion from Napoleonic France, a regiment of Preston Royal Volunteers had been raised. William Cross was commissioned Lieutenant in 1797 and Captain in 1798.

There was in Preston at this time a club, exclusively for gentlemen, with the odd title of the Oyster and Parched Pea Club. Its members, who were among the town's leading citizens, met weekly at each other's houses. The Club had many officers, such as Cellarius, who had to provide port of the first quality; Oystericus, who was in charge of the oysters; a Clerk of the Peas, an office always held by a member of the Gorst family, and a Rhymesmith. Such was William Cross, who had a great talent for verse. He is thought to be the author of the following, written in 1806.

Red Scar

'Yet undismayed amid the strife [in Europe]
Let us to festive joys give life
Nor mind yon tyrant fell.
Nelson has made the seas our own
Then gulp your well-fed oysters down
And give the French the shell!'

Mr Cross was a most welcome guest everywhere in the neighbourhood. He attended assemblies, plays and concerts, but was also deeply religious and attached to the Church of England.

By the time he moved into Winckley Street, William Cross had long ago fallen in love with the country around Red Scar and the Horse Shoe Bend of the 'sweet Ribble' as he called it. He bought Red Scar Cottage and spent all his weekends there, going to church at Grimsargh in the mornings, often walking home by Elston through the woods, and to church at Samlesbury – by boat – in the evenings. In 1813, when he was forty-two years of age, he married Ellen Chaffers of Liverpool. It was at this point that he took up residence permanently at Red Scar, having enlarged the original cottage into an Elizabethan-type house of considerable dimensions.

William and Ellen Cross enjoyed fourteen years of truly wedded bliss until, on a visit to Liverpool, William Cross caught a chill. Inflammation of the lungs developed and, as was the medical practice of the day, he was bled, literally to death. His widow was left with six children, the eldest of eleven years, the youngest of seven months.

Everyone in the town mourned his passing. William Cross is buried in the chancel of Grimsargh Church. It was his widow, Ellen, along with the trustees appointed by William Cross, who negotiated all the subsequent sales of plots of land in the Square, imposing the more specific and stringent conditions upon the purchasers. She died in 1849 and lies with her husband in the chancel of Grimsargh Church. Members of the Cross family lived on at Red Scar until the 1930s when it was demolished to build the Courtaulds factory.

AN EXAMPLE OF THE STRINGENT CONDITIONS DEMANDED BY ELLEN CROSS

Isaac Wilcockson was the owner and editor of the *Preston Chronicle* and, as a printer, published many works of local interest. He was also a founder member of Preston Gas Company, and of the Preston Waterworks. He lived at no. 12 Ribblesdale Place, directly opposite Camden Place.

On 26th October, 1844, he purchased from Ellen Cross of Red Scar a plot of land in Camden Place, the 'consideration' being £156 3s 4d on which he was to build two dwelling houses nos. 9 and 10 Camden Place. Behind these dwellings he was to build a stable, coach house and harness room for the use of the owners/occupiers of 9 and 10 Camden Place.

These houses were to be occupied as private dwelling houses only, and if they 'shall at any time thereafter be burnt down, pulled down, or destroyed the same when rebuilt shalt be built according to their former elevation and appearance.'

Isaac Wilcockson, at his own expense and to the satisfaction of the said Ellen Cross, must 'make form and flag with good Haslingden flags a footpath along the whole of the west side of the plot . . . must erect and forever maintain iron palisadoes along the whole of the west side of the Plot . . . 3ft 3ins high above the level of the adjoining footpath and of the same pattern as the palisadoes erected at the north end of a dwelling house in Latham Street belonging to Mr Richard Carr.'

'He must not permit the said Stable, Coach house and Harness Room to be used as a Livery Stable, Carter's Stable or in any other manner than as the Stable Coach house and Harness Room of a private gentleman. . . . He must use it in such a manner as not to be an annoyance to the owners or occupiers of any adjoining property.' 'Any breach of the conditions and Ellen Cross will apply to the High Court of Chancery for the County Palatine of Lancaster for any injunction to restrain or reform any such breach.'

THE ADDISONS

When Mr Cross took up residence at Red Scar, no. 7 Winckley Street was taken over by Mr John Addison, a barrister, and descendant of one of the oldest families in the history of Preston. In this rare photograph of a picture painted whilst the Addison family were at breakfast, Mrs Addison is seen presiding over the teapot, with her coachman, 'old' George Tyson, at her elbow. Her husband John, known as John Addison Senior, is seated to her right, whilst her son, John Addison Junior, stands by the fireplace, reading the *Preston Chronicle*. Her eldest son, Thomas Batty Addison, is seated cross-legged at the corner of the table, and over to the right her youngest son, Richard, completes the picture.

The Addison family at breakfast

Before coming to this house, the Addisons, like Mr Cross, had lived in Fishergate on the corner of Chapel Walks. The Addison family originated in 1622 at Maulds Meaburn in Westmorland, being of the same stock as the famous essayist, Joseph Addison. The family has an ancient role in Preston's history, the grandfather of John Addison Senior being Mayor in 1727 and 1735.

John Addison Senior and Agnes Batty were married on 13th September 1784. He was twenty-nine years of age; she was eighteen, and in the next twenty-five years, at the house in Fishergate, Mrs Addison bore her husband eleven children of whom only four survived to become adults. These were the three sons seen in the picture and one daughter, Susanna, who was born in November 1794 and died in December 1818, just before her second wedding anniversary and just after her twenty-fourth birthday.

By 1818 the Addisons were well-established in Winckley Square, and in her diary for the year 1821 Mrs Addison records many social occasions with neighbouring families. January was a very busy month: on the 5th a 'Party of ladies at home'; on the 18th 'At Mrs Fieldings'; on the 19th 'Party of Gentlemen'; on the 29th 'Mrs Gorsts'; (that would be Mrs Edward Gorst); on the 30th 'Mrs J. Gorsts'. In February she visited Mifs Dalton and on December 10th there was a 'Dinner Party of 12', whilst on December 27th 'Mr Aspden's Rout'.

The Addisons were great travellers. In this same year of 1821, Mr and Mrs Addison Senior and their youngest son Richard went on a long holiday to France and the Netherlands, their journeys always being recorded in diaries and sketch-books.

Winckley Square c.1825, drawing by Anne Agnes Addison

Thomas Batty Addison and John Addison Junior were, like their father, barristers, and they conducted a very busy legal practice from their home in Winckley Street. On 21st June 1823, John Addison Junior married Louisa Caroline Mary Anne Hulton, and on 1st August 1824, a daughter Anne Agnes, was born to them. Only a year later, on 20th August 1825, her mother died, aged twenty-six. John Addison never remarried and Anne Agnes in her infancy was brought up by Aunt Charlotte, the wife of her uncle Richard Addison at the house in Winckley Square. When Anne Agnes was twelve years of age she was sent to a private school in Bryanston Square, London, where she remained many years, studying hard and conscientiously and making many visits of a cultural nature.

On 15th October 1845, the twenty-one year old Anne Agnes Addison was married to Major John ffolliot Crofton who was forty-five years of age. The marriage had been opposed by her father because of this great disparity in age, and since the Addisons were so prominent a family in the town, the event had 'for some days previous been the general theme of conversation. By nine o'clock, Fishergate, Church Street and Winckley Street exhibited signs of unusual excitement.'

Winckley Square, east side, 1863, photograph by Robert Pateson

'Many were flocking to Winckley Street to obtain a glimpse of the bridal party as they stepped into the carriages, of which there were nine in number. A crowded Parish Church saw Miss Addison arrive attired in a splendid white watered-silk gown covered with a rich lace veil, which was suspended by a wreath of orange blossoms.' There were five bridesmaids, 'all elegantly attired in white satin dresses, covered with white net. At the conclusion of the ceremony as Major and Mrs Crofton entered the first carriage they were welcomed by a merry peal from the church bells – a large amount of silver was scattered among the crowd in the street, and the party returned to the house of Mr Addison where an elegant déjeuner had been prepared. To this repast, about thirty ladies and gentlemen sat down. The domestics were not forgotten on the occasion, for in the evening they were allowed, with their friends, to enjoy themselves in singing and dancing, which they kept up with great spirit, to a late hour.' The marriage proved to be a happy one and was blessed with four sons and two daughters. The early years were in Preston, the later ones in London.

Anne Agnes's father, John Addison, continued to live at no. 7 Winckley Street with his elder brother, Thomas Batty, until some time after 1851 when they built and moved to no. 23 Winckley Square. Throughout their lives both these gentlemen were closely associated with the town of Preston. John Addison was twice the Mayor, in 1832 and 1843, and in 1847 he was appointed a County Court Judge. He was a very kindly man who always strove most anxiously to arrive at an honest decision. His death came very suddenly on 14th July 1859, at the age of sixty-eight years.

His elder brother, Thomas Batty Addison, lived on until 1874. He was described in his obituary as 'a man of strong will and firm purpose . . . a feature in his character which frequently brought him into personal conflict with other public men in the town.' Such a man was Joseph Livesey. On the introduction of the new Poor Law Act in 1834, Thomas Batty Addison had been appointed the first Chairman of the Preston Union and had, from the first, advocated the building of a Union Workhouse for the relief of the in-door poor.

John Addison with his daughter, Mrs Ann Agnes Crofton, 1846,
photograph attributed to Silas Eastham

The whole town was up in arms against this proposal which Mr Joseph Livesey opposed with vigour. Long discussions took place both in print and in public places, and thirty years elapsed before the Poor Law authorities adopted Mr Addison's plan. A Union Workhouse in Fulwood was decided upon and Mr Addison laid the foundation stone. The building was opened in December 1868 but Joseph Livesey continued to oppose Thomas Batty Addison. 'His views and mine as to the character and merits of the poor', he wrote, 'were so utterly at variance . . . I knew their condition from actual visitation and he did not. He was very severe, and I was lenient.' In that workhouse, in the name of 'classification', husbands, wives and children were all separated from each other. 'My heart has bled many a time to see the poor pleading for a small pittance of outdoor relief. Mr Addison's response was uniformly "the house".'

Thomas Batty Addison c.1857, photograph by Thomas Ogle

On 24th March 1832, Thomas Batty Addison was appointed the Recorder of Preston, an office he held until his death. He was also the Chairman of the Preston Court of Quarter Sessions, an appointment he resigned in April 1874, when he was eighty-six years of age. Two months later, on 6th June 1874, he died.

When Thomas Batty Addison was nearly eighty-three years of age, Anthony Hewittson described him in *Preston Town Council Portraits* as 'a diminutive, fresh-featured gentlemen, wonderfully active for his age. He has an intensely sharp eye in his head, has a brisk temper, soon kindles up into a lively mood, stoops considerably, always walked with his hands behind him; has a sanguine and rather fierce disposition; likes castigating rogues and vagabonds; has precious little respect for the brains of common jurymen, and once nearly got into a mess by calling a parcel of them, who wouldn't use their reason, dunces or blockheads; walks in a trotting sort of way, and blows his cheeks often . . . sits with remarkable endurance at the court house during sessions of business, but persists in going late to work and keeping everybody waiting; is about the clearest headed gentleman that we know of, for his years; has a small, round, quaint looking head, full of mental strength and shrewdness; is vivacious, witty, and buoyant in spirit; is well versed in law and general literature; has led a life of thorough rectitude and independence of action; has, like his brother John, been a great peacemaker and settler of disputes and grievances in private life; has been of much use to the town and the county; and merits what we cheerfully give him – our highest reverence and esteem.'

Richard, the younger son of the Addison family, did not live locally, but was engaged in the cotton industry in Holywell, Wales. After his death at the early age of forty-seven, his widow Charlotte lived with John and Thomas Batty Addison in Winckley Square.

NICHOLAS GRIMSHAW

Another characteristic shared by the early residents of Winckley Square was that they all played a major part in the life of Preston. Nicholas Grimshaw certainly did that. He was born in 1757 and educated for the law. Before coming to Winckley Square he lived in Church Street, almost opposite Grimshaw Street, which was so named to honour his family. There is an old story about an incident which took place during his residence there.

'He was fond of the violin and one market day, while playing the instrument, there chanced to come along the street a countryman. The door of the house, or the window of the room in which Mr Grimshaw was playing, was open and the countryman, knowing that fiddle-playing was no uncommon thing on a market day in a public place, fancied this was such a place; so in he went – walked right into the room when Mr Grimshaw was playing, took a seat and knocked on the table with his fist for a waiter to come and take his order. Mr Grimshaw quietly walked toward him and asked what he wanted. "A glass of ale", was the reply. Mr Grimshaw good-humoredly rang the bell, and forthwith appeared one of the servants, who was requested to bring a glass of ale. It was drawn and brought. "What's to pay?" inquired the man. "Nothing", answered Mr Grimshaw, whereupon thanks were freely rendered, followed by "Good health" and the speedy supping of the ale. The man then got up and quietly walked out, having no idea he had been in the private residence of one of the principal gentlemen of the town, but simply that he had encountered a generous "publican" in his own "hotel".'

Nicholas Grimshaw had a very lucrative legal practice and held most of the public appointments in the town. When the regiment of Preston Royal Volunteers was raised in 1797 he was appointed Colonel, and in 1802, the year of his first Guild mayoralty, the officers of the Regiment presented his Lady with a full-length portrait of their Colonel, as a mark of their respect. This now hangs in the Regimental Museum in Stanley Street [now in storage in the Harris Museum]. He made such a success of the Guild of 1802 that a grateful Corporation presented him with a magnificent set of silver plate. An account of that Guild records that after the Gentlemen's Procession on the Monday, 'Mr Grimshaw, the Mayor, entertained the gentlemen with a sumptuous dinner at his house in Winckley Place. The Mayoress likewise entertained the ladies on the following day.'

Although he lived such a busy professional life, Nicholas Grimshaw found time to indulge in many cultural pursuits. He was President of the Preston Musical Society and of the Preston Assembly, and held the office of Speaker in the Oyster and Parched Pea Club.

Lithograph of a portrait of Nicholas Grimshaw by James Lonsdale

But great tragedy befell during his second Guild mayoralty in 1822, when his two sons, Nicholas Charles, aged twenty, and George Henry, aged seventeen, were drowned in a boating accident in the River Ribble. They and two friends, who also drowned, had been celebrating the birthday of King George IV. In the records of that Guild it is recorded that 'Mr Grimshaw bore the loss with Christian fortitude; but the Mayoress was so much overcome by the sudden stroke that she felt unequal to the exacting duties of the position of Lady Mayoress; but she found an admirable substitute in her daughter, Mrs Atkinson, wife of Robert Atkinson, Esqr., of Studdy Lodge near Lancaster. The Mayoress, Mrs Grimshaw, was a lady of the finest character, much beloved by all classes for her gentleness and generous charity, and her absence from the Guild ceremonies gave rise to universal regret for the unfortunate cause of it.'

We can still see the name of Nicholas Grimshaw on the inscription over the entrance to the old Corn Exchange, which we call the Public Hall [now the Corn Exchange public house]. This was erected for the Guild of 1822.

Nicholas Grimshaw died in January 1838, aged eighty. His gravestone is preserved in the grass verge of Preston Parish Church in Church Street.

Here are deposited the Remains

of

NICHOLAS CHARLES GRIMSHAW Aged 20 Years
& GEORGE HENRY GRIMSHAW Aged 17 Years
(the 3rd & 6th Sons of NICHOLAS GRIMSHAW
Esqr. of this Town & ESTHER MARY his Wife)

Who were Drowned in the River Ribble on

the 24th Day of April, A.D. 1822

Also the Remains of the above

named NICHOLAS GRIMSHAW Esqr.

Who departed this life on the 17th Day

of January 1838 Aged 80 Years.

Also the Remains of the above

named ESTHER MARY GRIMSHAW

Relict of the above named

NICHOLAS GRIMSHAW Esqr.

Who departed this life on the

26th day of December 1855

Aged 86 Years.

THE REV ROGER CARUS WILSON

The Rev Roger Carus Wilson was Vicar of Preston from 1817, when he was only 25 years of age, to 1839. In the years 1830–31 he built the present no. 7 Winckley Square.

Due to the growth of the cotton industry in Preston and the consequent increase in the town's population, his incumbency was remarkable for the great increase in churches built to answer the spiritual needs of the workers. The Rev Roger Carus Wilson was responsible for the building of five new churches within the Borough of Preston. These were St Peter's in 1825, St Paul's in 1826, Christ Church in 1836, St Mary's in 1838 and St Thomas's in 1839. He also purchased, in 1838, the Primitive Episcopal Church which became St James's, and in Ashton, then beyond the Preston boundary, he built St Andrew's Church.

The Rev Roger Carus Wilson died very suddenly on Sunday afternoon, 15th December 1839. He was a very energetic man, with an impressive and beautiful style of delivery who enjoyed the esteem and affection of his congregation. To that congregation in 1839 he appeared to be a very healthy man with a long life before him, and so stunned were they to hear the news of his death 'that for some time the rumour was not credited, and Winckley Square was, until about four o'clock, completely thronged by inquirers, anxious to learn every particular of the melancholy circumstance.' These were dramatic indeed.

During the previous week the Vicar had been much exposed to the cold and inclement weather, and on Saturday afternoon, went to bed with what he believed to be a slight cold. Dr Moore was consulted and confirmed this. The Vicar slept soundly till Sunday morning and, feeling better, decided to get up and preach at Grimsargh. He was, however, to stay in bed and again fell asleep until between two and three o'clock in the afternoon when he awoke, feeling worse. He asked his wife to send for a neighbour and when the lady arrived she 'immediately perceived that the lamented gentleman was on the eve of dissolution'. She voiced her fears and the Vicar asked that the Rev Thomas Clark of Christ Church be sent for, these being 'the last words he ever spoke'. He died about 3.30 p.m. just before the arrival of the Rev Clark who had been preaching to his congregation when summoned.

On the south wall of Preston Parish Church there is an elaborate memorial to the Rev Roger Carus Wilson 'erected to his memory by those who loved him living and mourned him dead'. At the base of this memorial are shown in relief the five new churches erected through his exertions within the Borough of Preston.

SAMUEL LEACH 1829–1923

In the Harris Reference Library there is a book I have only recently discovered, entitled *Old Age Reminiscences* by Samuel Leach. He wrote this in 1916, when he was eighty-six years of age, and it begins: 'I was born on the 5th December 1829, in a house, (one of a terrace of three), on the lower, which is the south side, of Winckley Square, Preston.'

Samuel was the youngest son of Thomas Leach, hosier and draper, whose business premises were at 130 and 131 Fishergate, though an early trade directory gives the address as 1 Cheapside. This is born out by the front page of issue No. 24 of *The Struggle* which shows Preston Obelisk where the 'perpetual auctions' were 'A Sign of the Times' and where the name 'LEACH' can be seen on the shop at the top of Cheapside.

5 Camden Place

It was when Samuel was about five years of age that his father acquired one of the few vacant plots of land in the Square and built two houses, closely adjoining that in which they already lived. One of these was for his own occupation and the other for a tenancy; both houses were in Camden Place, but Mr Leach's house, being on the corner, with the front door in Camden Place, had many rooms which overlooked the Square. With the house went a large garden plot in the central area of the Square which could be seen from the drawing room windows and from the bedrooms above. This garden was a source of delight to the youngsters in the family and also provided a most plentiful supply of fruit, flowers and vegetables for the household. The younger boys had plots to care for but most of the gardening was done by their elder sister who was very devoted to this task.

The main feature inside the house was the wealth of store-rooms! Favourite amongst these was the one in the dining room which was very large and shelved from top to bottom. It was the boys' sanctum sanctorum and contained boxes of toffee, ginger-bread, parkin, groceries, string, joinery tools of every description and, at Christmas, raised mince pies.

It was a lovely house in which to play hide and seek, containing only two living rooms, one on each side of the front door; the dining room to the left, looking into Camden Place; the drawing room to the right, with two windows to the Square.

Samuel's parents had their bedroom on the first floor; in winter over the dining room for warmth, and in summer over the drawing room which faced north. Both rooms had fine old four-poster beds with curtains to draw all round. Other bedrooms on this first floor were those of Samuel's only sister and the servants. The boys' bedrooms were on the second floor.

The house was cellared throughout, there being a larder, washing cellar with a huge mangle, and coal and wine cellars. Candles were used for illumination, two in each sitting room on ordinary occasions, but four on 'state' occasions. For night lights in a case of sickness or otherwise they had small wicks floating on the top of oil in large glasses, 'much the shape and size of a rose bowl'.

Samuel Leach describes the weekly ritual of doing the household washing. As boys, he and his brothers were allowed to sit up until the watchman's first round, 'and to see him cloaked up to the chin, a dark mysterious figure with a lantern on wet and windy nights, was quite awe inspiring. It was part of the watchman's duties to knock with his stick on the wall just under the maids' bedroom window and so awake them, and this took place from on Monday mornings at half-past two o'clock for the wash, so that by the time we came down to breakfast we often saw the clothes, already dried, being brought in from the grass plot at the bottom of our garden.' 'What', he asks in 1916, 'would the maids today have to say to this? And yet we kept them as a rule for periods of six, eight or even ten years or until they left us to marry.'

Before the age of six, Samuel was sent to a mixed boys' and girls' school kept by a Miss Foster in Charles Street, 'now swallowed up in the Station buildings'. At eight years of age he went to the Grammar School in Stoneygate, this being moved in 1842 to 'fine new buildings in Cross Street, in the same block as the museum, library and lecture room of the Literary and Philosophical Society; many of my dinner hours were spent reading in this library, as the family had tickets admitting us to all the privileges in connection with this Society.'

At the Grammar School he was required to learn 'for night work' thirty to fifty lines at a time of Latin and Greek. 'I used to sit half-way up our stairs at home, where we had a convenient gas jet, night after night, learning Latin by heart.'

Amongst his principal 'playfellows' were James Brown, brother of the future Sir Charles Brown, and John Rofe, son of the gas engineer, whose 'principal use was his having access to the Gas Works, his father being chief man there, and our delight was to dance about on the top of the big gasometers before they filled for the night's use, and no dancing floor was ever so springy as those elastic tops.'

Samuel and his friends had little in the way of entertainment as we know it today. They went, in winter evenings, for tea to each others' homes where they had games, piano music or singing. They went, also, to an occasional lecture, this being a great period for lectures and sermons, but never to the theatre or concert room.

The family holidayed in Lytham or Blackpool and, to get there, travelled in a hired covered green market cart. The journey to Lytham would take fully two hours, and an hour longer to Blackpool! Samuel well remembers getting up at six o'clock one morning when he was eight years old, to see the first train start from Preston. That was in 1838 when the North Union Railway began running trains as far as Wigan.

In June 1845, Samuel elected to go into business with his brother John in Manchester, rather than go to university. There he remained for five years, working long hours, from 8.30 a.m. till 7.30 p.m. every weekday. He and his brother went every fortnight from Saturday afternoon to Monday morning to the old home at Preston. Their father always met them at the station. Thomas Leach, although born in Clitheroe, had been almost a life-long resident in Preston and worked constantly for the town's welfare. Among the many positions he occupied were: director of the gas company from its formation in 1815; director of the Preston Banking Company; director of the Steam Saw Mill; a large interest in the Ribble Navigation Company; trustee of the Savings Bank; local treasurer to two of the large missionary societies; and for some years a member of the Town Council, with an offer of the mayoralty, which he declined.

In June 1850, Samuel left Manchester to join his other brother, Joseph, a cotton-broker in Liverpool, becoming his partner at the close of the year when he was twenty-one. Business hours were shorter in Liverpool, being from nine to five or five-thirty. Joseph and Samuel still spent occasional weekends at Preston.

In 1851, Samuel had a wonderful time visiting the Great Exhibition at the Crystal Palace in London with his Aunt Cowell who seems to have been a very sprightly old lady. In August 1855, he was married, we are not told to whom, except that she was a bridesmaid to Samuel's sister-in-law. With this marriage Samuel ends his story, leaving his children to complete it. He died on 12th March 1923, being in his 94th year.

THOMAS MILLER

In 1851, or thereabouts, the Addisons left 7 Winckley Street to live on the western side of the Square at no. 23, which is now Winckleys on the Square [now the Chop House]. The house in Winckley Street was then taken over by Mr Thomas Miller, of the cotton firm, Horrockses Miller, the most powerful cotton manufacturer in the town. Whilst resident there he built his own splendid house on the garden of no. 7 – a house which was later to become the Junior Park School.

Alderman Thomas Miller, 1862 Preston Guild, photograph by Samuel Oglesby

Mr and Mrs Miller had two sons and three daughters, and their house was well staffed with servants. In the census for 1861, there were seven members of the family and nine servants. In 1871 there were six members of the family and eleven servants! These were kitchen maid, house maid, under-house maid, a German governess, butler, footman, groom, two ladies' maids, one under-ladies' maid and one cook!

The Miller residence [now Blackthorn Homes]

It was Alderman Thomas Miller who gave to Preston the land for Miller Park. That was in 1864, and in 1865 he died, aged 54 years. His funeral was a tremendous affair. 'The members of the Corporation assembled at the Corn Exchange and walked to the deceased's residence in Winckley Square. Before nine o'clock a vast concourse of people had already gone there. The bells of the Parish Church rang a muffled peal, flags were at half mast, shops were closed and blinds drawn. Three thousand of Mr Miller's workmen lined the funeral route, and as the cortège passed, fell in step behind it.' Mr Miller also owned a house at West Beach, Lytham, and he was interred in the graveyard of St John's Church there. Some of the work people caught trains to Lytham, and so followed their late master to his last resting place.

RICHARD NEWSHAM

A great friend of Thomas Miller was Richard Newsham who, for fifty-three years, lived at no. 1 Winckley Square. He was a member of a wealthy banking family who had the good fortune to invest in John Horrocks. He too was trained for the law and devoted to public service, being a County and a Borough Magistrate. He built schools at his own expense and was warmly attached to the Church of England. He placed memorials in St James's Church 'for my good Father and Mother and for my devoted and beloved Wife'. He even designed his own memorial, a large stained-glass window of which he wrote, 'I should wish this window to be taken as monumental to myself . . . it will remain, a lasting testimony of my love and veneration for God's House. and of my Gratitude and Thankfulness for all His gracious dealings with me.' Ironically, the church has been declared 'redundant'; all its treasures have been auctioned off, and the building razed to the ground.

Richard Newsham c.1857, photograph by Thomas Ogle

During his lifetime, Mr Newsham amassed a large art collection which, on his death in January 1883, he bequeathed to the Corporation of Preston. In due course this formed the basis of the art collection at the Harris Museum and Art Gallery, the foundation stone of which had been laid at the Guild of 1882. That collection can still be seen at the Harris.

LETTERS TO THE EDITOR IN 1854

NUISANCE
To the Editor of the *Guardian*

SIR, – A great nuisance in Winckley-square and Ribblesdale-place is occasioned by grooms daily exercising horses in the afternoon, when people are out taking exercise. My wife and myself are timid people, and the other week we met five in a row, the horses capering and kicking. May I suggest, not wishing to give offence, that there are many suitable places about town, such as the Marsh by the new road, or the Moor Park, far preferable to the Square. My horses are exercised in a different part, without annoying anyone. A word from the masters to their servants would secure this nuisance being abated.

Yours & c

AN OLD INHABITANT.

Jan 30. 1854.

Preston Guardian, 4th February 1854, page 6.

POLICE REPORT
To the Editor of the *Guardian*

SIR, – My thanks are especially due for your kindness in having inserted my last letter. The effect has been marvellous. A policeman has been placed on duty all day, patrolling, and very few beggars are to be seen.

I would suggest a continuance of this part of the town (Winckley Square and Avenham) being properly watched, which is no more than the inhabitants are entitled to. Being a family man, my servant has other duties to perform than to be going to the bell every minute.

When Mr Gibbons is settled, let him have a brass plate on his door, that strangers may know where to find him. The same remark applies to the inspector.

The beggars now assemble from Mr Addison's corner, up to Avenham, and from that point more than any other continue to annoy people.

I am, yours A CONSTANT READER.

Preston, 1st February 1854.

Preston Guardian, 4th February 1854, page 6.

SIR CHARLES BROWN

Many of us will remember the old Preston Royal Infirmary. How many, I wonder, can recall Brown Ward there, and know why it was so called? It was to honour Sir Charles Brown, a Preston doctor who lived for all but ten years of his life at no. 27 Winckley Square. He was born there in 1836, educated at the Grammar School in Cross Street, did his medical training in London, and, on qualifying, returned to Preston to be House Surgeon at the Dispensary in Fishergate. The Preston Royal Infirmary was opened in 1870 and Dr Brown was appointed a member of staff. He remained there until 1922, being *Sixty-Four Years a Doctor* – this being the title of a book he wrote when he was eighty-six years of age.

His father had also been a doctor: Dr Robert Brown, born in 1800. His medical training, in a country practice, had been very hard, with visits done on horseback. He

Dr Charles Brown

had to wash, in all weathers, in a stone trough in the stable yard, unlike his son who, at no. 27 Winckley Square, enjoyed the luxury of a 'beautiful, full-length marble bath, combined with a shower bath, supplied with hot and cold water, and a wash-basin, similarly furnished.'

In his book *Sixty-Four Years a Doctor* Dr Brown recalls his early years at no. 27 Winckley Square, where he lived with his parents, two brothers and four sisters. The domestic staff consisted of a governess, nurse, cook, parlourmaid and housemaid. Each servant had her own particular duty. The cook had to prepare four meals daily for the fourteen people. The parlourmaid waited upon everyone except the two youngest children and the other servants. She also had to answer the doorbell day and night. The housemaid, with the help of the parlourmaid, had to make all the beds and attend to most of the rooms. The washing was done by the cook, housemaid, parlourmaid and nurse. They were called for the purpose every Monday morning at one o'clock, one and a half hours earlier than the maids were called at the Leach household for the same task, and by that same night watchman who patrolled the neighbourhood and called the hour and the state of the weather.

There was no gas in any of the bedrooms and coals had to be carried up from the cellar. The servants had to clean both the inside and outside of the windows because there were no window cleaners then. Lowest paid was the nurse who received £8 a year. 'The coachman, a married man, had 14s. a week and a bonus of £2 on Christmas Day, Samuel Cave was the coachman. He had four sons. . . . The coachman's wife and my good mother were examples in character generally, and household management in particular.'

Dr Brown was always concerned about the bad health of the town and felt that the inadequate domestic training given to young girls who had been put in the mill at an early age was largely to blame, since when they married they made very inadequate wives and mothers. He constantly urged the authorities in Preston to make domestic science a compulsory subject in elementary schools and he finally succeeded, which is why in 1896 the School of Domestic Science opened in Glover's Court.

At Preston Royal Infirmary he defrayed the expense of building a new operating theatre at a cost of £2,700, provided money for structural improvements and equipment which kept the Infirmary thoroughly up to date in every respect. He greatly valued 'his' nurses and gave them a free day out in Fleetwood and Blackpool every year.

Whenever important people visited the town he delighted to entertain them at his home in Winckley Square, always showing off to them the things in Preston of which he was most proud – Preston Royal Infirmary, the Harris Museum and Art Gallery, and the Harris Orphanage.

Dr Brown, who never married, died in November 1925. An announcement placed outside his house read 'Sir Charles Brown passed peacefully away at 8.35 this morning.' He was cremated in Manchester and, at the same time as the service there, a full civic memorial service was held in Preston Parish Church for Preston's 'Grand Old Man'.

EDITH RIGBY

Another remarkable resident of Winckley Square was a lady – born Edith Rayner, at no. 1 Pole Street, she was the sister of Dr Arthur Rayner who founded the X-ray Department at Preston Royal Infirmary. Just before her twenty-first birthday in 1893, she married Dr Charles Rigby and they set up house at no. 28 Winckley Square, next door to Dr Brown. Edith had always been unusual. She identified with the poor cotton workers and mill girls she had known as a child, rather than with the wealthy, middle-class residents of Winckley Square.

Edith Rigby

Mrs Rigby was strikingly beautiful, tall, with wheat-gold hair and blue eyes. She wore extraordinary dresses, like blue sacking, with heavy, amber-coloured beads on chains. Though she was clearly authoritative, she never raised her voice, but gave an overwhelming impression of gentleness. Always concerned for the under-dog, Mrs Rigby founded, in 1899, a night-school and recreation club for working girls in St Peter's school in Brook Street.

She inquired, much to the annoyance of her Winckley Square neighbours, into the working conditions of maids who, in her own house, were treated as equals. One family, who lived a few doors away, were so incensed by this that they called on her one evening and told her plainly that if she couldn't alter her ways she had better leave the neighbourhood.

Her courage and idealism never wavered, for she then became involved in the suffrage movement and, in 1907, formed a Preston branch of the Women's Social and Political Union with herself as secretary. All the organisation of this branch and its early meetings were held at no. 28 Winckley Square, and when important members of the movement visited the town, that is where they stayed. Many dinner parties were held there with the ladies wearing their ceremonial long white dresses and the sashes of white corded ribbon edged with purple and green.

Mrs Rigby and her friends were part of the militant branch of the suffragettes, and she was blamed for the tarring of Lord Derby's statue in Miller Park. Although this was her idea and she arranged it all, she did not actually commit the awful deed. She did, however, burn down Lord Leverhulme's wooden bungalow on Rivington Pike and throw a bomb into the Liverpool Cotton Exchange. She was imprisoned many times for these offences, and suffered the terrible forcible feeding.

On one occasion, when the police called at no. 28 Winckley Square to re-arrest her under the 'Cat and Mouse' Act, she made her escape to Ireland from the rear of the house, wearing workman's clothes and riding a bicycle!

Edith Rigby was an extremely brave woman, both physically and morally, and you can read her story in the book *My Aunt Edith*, written by her niece, the poet, Phoebe Hesketh, to whom I am indebted for all the foregoing. Here, also is a poem by Phoebe Hesketh which is a fitting end to my brief account of Edith Rigby. It is entitled, 'The Ghost of Ribblesdale Place' and as you read it, remember that Phoebe Hesketh was the daughter of Dr Arthur Rayner and their home was no. 9 Ribblesdale Place.

The Ghost of Ribblesdale Place, Preston

Where are they gone
who lived in the street where I was born?
After the vans moved out
developers, accountants, insurance brokers
moved in with fresh paint
and prosperous copper name-plates.
No flowers or face at the windows.

The houses are still the same; fronts to the street
gardened backs sloping to park and river.
But where are the two Miss Horrocks'[1]
wearing lavender on a tidy lawn,
white-haired admiring hollyhocks?
And the jolly Miller sisters,[2] privet-screened,
spilling jokes across a crochet tablecloth?
And childless Mrs Riddeall bidding children
to pancake parties?

At the leafy corner, hidden by a hawthorn,
the Sellers[3] lived secluded –
she was tall, wore feathered hats, and died
when Benjamin, their pride, was killed in France.
The ladies of the Place
whispered among the tea cups and were shocked,
but not outraged as by the suffragette,
my aunt,[4] who threatened nearby Winckley Square
with disrepute,
tarring Lord Derby's statue, planting bombs
in a flower-bed, burning the summer home
of a local millionaire.[5]

She who seven times had been in gaol,
force-fed, beaten-up and bruised, had bled
fighting for their rights,
she who was shunned and asked to leave the Square:
Strangeways was her proper place, they said.

But what of our house, solid Number Nine
with my father's name[6] half rubbed away in brass,
where X-rays sparked and crackled, and we two,
the noisy ones, were banished to the garden?

I see my younger sister in the grass
threading a daisy-chain
while I, impatient, spur the horse-on-wheels
down to the cherry tree
inside the high wall topped with jagged glass.

On fretful wet days, pressed to the nursery window,
we looked down to the Ribble sliding slow
under the railway bridge, counted the trains
dragoned with sparks and smoking plumes, that roared
black thunder over the arches.

Here I linger, peopling the Place
with all who lived here, all who've made me me –
parents, aunts, and friends, and younger sister.
It's late; the lights flick on; the failing sun
touches the roofs and windows of the lost.
Shadows reach me waiting here alone
among the living – it's I who am the ghost.

Phoebe Hesketh

[1] Of the Horrockses, Crewdson, & Co firm.
[2] Sisters of Dr Tom Miller, leading dental surgeon.
[3] Dr Sellars, physician on the staff of Preston Royal Infirmary.
[4] Mrs Edith Rigby, who started the suffrage movement in Preston.
[5] Sir William Lever (later Lord Leverhulme).
[6] Dr Arthur Rayner, first director of Preston Royal Infirmary's X-ray Department, opened in 1904.

THREE HANDSOME BUILDINGS

What were, perhaps, the handsomest group of buildings stood at the corner of Winckley Square and Cross Street. Hardwick, in his *History of the Borough of Preston*, written in 1857, refers to them as 'one of the chief architectural ornaments of the town'. They were the Winckley Club, on the eastern side of the Square, the Literary and Philosophical Institution which adjoined the Club and stood on the corner of Cross Street, extending into that street and, beyond that, the Grammar School, all of which have been demolished and replaced by modern buildings.

An engraving of the Winckley Club and Dr Shepherd's Library
(formerly the Literary and Philosophical Institution)

The Winckley Club

The predecessor to the Winckley Club was the Gentlemen's Coffee Room, said to be a large building situated at the Church Street end of Lancaster Road and erected between 1822 and 1826. At a meeting held on 25th May 1844, with Mr Thomas Miller in the chair, it was resolved 'That a Society be now formed for erecting a News Room and Billiards Room on the east side of Winckley Square' and that 'a fund of two thousand pounds be raised for the purposes of the Society in shares of twenty-five pounds each.'

Mr Peter Caterall was appointed secretary, and Mr Robert Lawe, treasurer, who, along with Messrs Miller, Paul Catterall, William Ainsworth, John Winstanley and John Stevenson comprised the Building Committee. Mr Welch was requested to prepare the detailed drawings and specification. The land was purchased from Mrs Cross and the Club opened on 1st May, 1846.

The shareholders alone were to have the management of the Club and alone be entitled to the profits and bear the losses arising therefrom. Eventually, there were a hundred shares owned by eighty-two shareholders. Annual subscribers were also admitted and 'Country' subscribers at half the rate of ordinary ones.

The Newsroom was a very important feature of the Club and at every Annual General Meeting, from the very first one, there was an auction of newspapers and periodicals for the ensuing year. This meant that the highest bidder could purchase every issue of a newspaper or periodical for the coming year after it had been made available to the Club members in the Newsroom for a stipulated time. It was then delivered to the purchaser and became his property. Some papers, however, were filed and kept by the Club.

The Newsroom was to be open every day in the week from eight o'clock in the morning until eleven o'clock in the evening, though the first 'club keeper', William Ward, 'having inquired at what Hour the Newsroom should be closed on a Sunday evening the Committee informed him that no objection would be made to closing it on that day at ten o'clock if no member of the Club should then be present' (Committee Meeting 16th May 1846).

The Billiard Room was to be open 'every day in the week (except Sundays) during the same hours and until any game which may be in play at eleven o'clock be finished'. For its members, exclusively gentlemen, which included the wealthy cotton and other manufacturers, professional men, clergymen and officers of the military from Fulwood Barracks, the Club was a very comfortable place; for its servants, an exacting one.

The first club keeper, William Ward, was given the weekly wage of 18s [90p] and allowed 10s [50p] per week for cleaning the Club rooms. William Dunderdale was engaged as his assistant at the weekly wage of 5s [25p] and given 'a Suit of Clothes and a Hat, provided his Father will engage him for a twelve Month at least. Hours of attendance from 8 o'clock a.m. to 9 o'clock p.m.' (Committee Meeting 15th July 1846).

There were always difficulties in collecting the money for games of billiards, especially from the military who had a habit of leaving Preston without notice. Such sums were often written off. Subscriptions, too, were always slow to come in and it was often resolved, 'That the Club Keeper be sent to each Shareholder and Subscriber to request immediate payment.'

Below are some interesting extracts from the early minute books.

7th January 1850
The thermometer having been stolen from the Newsroom a new one is to be bought.

6th June 1850
The Marker to be allowed to live with his family in the cellar and be allowed coal, water and gas for the room during the pleasure of the Committee – for this 4/- [20p] to be deducted from his wages.

6th January 1851
Resolved that a Notice be put up in the Newsroom and Billiard Room regarding information from any Gentleman as to the Party who has taken the *Examiner* Newspaper out of the Room on three several occasions.

4th July 1853
That the Officers of the several Regiments which may be stationed at the Barracks have free access to the Newsroom.

2nd January 1854
That the Secretary do put up a notice requesting Gentlemen not to play at Billiards with their walking sticks.

3rd November 1856
Mr Peter Caterall having preferred a complaint against the Club Keeper with reference to his keeping Poultry on the Club Premises the Keeper was directed to discontinue keeping them.

11th May 1857
The charges for Billiards be for every Game played by daylight 4d. [1.6p] and by Gaslight 6d. [2.4p] for a Game of 50 and for a 24 Game one half of the above. That the charge for Pyramid Pool be the same as for a 50 Game of Billiards. That Gentlemen are requested before leaving the Billiard Room to see that the Games are entered in the Book by the Marker and the Charges for the same.

6th July 1857
The Club Keeper has reported to the Committee that the *Manchester Guardian* has several times been taken from the Newsroom and on Thursday last *The Times* was also taken. Members of the Committee and the Club Keeper to 'use their best endeavours to find out the parties taking the same'.

9th February 1860
That the Secretary be requested to forward the usual notice to the Officers of the 3rd Royal Lancs. Militia of their having the entries and privileges of the Club.

3rd March 1862
That the Secretary do write to Mr Hebden for 3/- [15p] the price of a Pack of Cards destroyed by him.

It was not until the mid-1950s that the wives of members were admitted to the Club as 'lady subscribers', though they could attend the lectures and private parties held at the Club.

Always a male preserve was the mid-day luncheon, partaken of chiefly by members of the medical profession, but also by solicitors and professional men whose business premises were close by. Increasingly the various hospitals in the town came to provide their own dining rooms and so there was a sad falling-off in attendance at Winckley Square where the dining room ran at a loss for some time.

As the Winckley Club was first proposed in 1844 its centenary year fell during World War II. So it was not until Saturday 15th January 1949, that it was possible to celebrate the event with a centenary dinner. Reproduced on the next page is the menu for that occasion, bearing on the back the signatures of many who were present.

In 1964 the Club was approached to sell its premises for re-development along with the Corporation-owned site of the old Grammar School and Dr Shepherd's Library, and it was felt by the majority of the membership that this was an opportunity to launch the Club into the twentieth century. It was agreed to sell the premises in Winckley Square and to purchase Moor Park Villa on Garstang Road which was intended to be a new Winckley Club worthy of the high standard of its predecessor. On May Day 1965 a farewell repast was partaken of. On the back of the menu card was printed:

> Extract from the Minutes of a Meeting held at the Preston Subscription Room on 25th May 1844.
>
> Present: Mr Miller (Chairman), Mr John Addison, Mr Paul Catterall, Mr Segar, Mr Peter Caterall, Mr Walmsley, Mr Thomas Harris, Mr William Ainsworth, Mr Horrocks, Mr John Catterall, Mr F. C. Harris, Mr Riley, Mr Marshall, Mr John Gradwell, Mr Ewings, Mr Goudy.
>
> RESOLVED: (1) That a Society be now formed for erecting a Newsroom and Billiard Room on the east side of Winckley Square in Preston on the plot of land between the house and premises now occupied by Henry Miller Esquire and a plot of land on the south thereof belonging to John Addison Esquire and this meeting now sanctions the purchase of the said land on behalf of this Society.
>
> (2) That a fund of two thousand pounds be raised for the purpose of the Society in Shares of Twenty Five Pounds each.

In March 1966, the Club re-opened in beautiful premises at Moor Park Villa on Garstang Road where, alongside the modern furnishings, were relics of the old Club: a grandfather clock in the vestibule, and on the first floor landing, leather chairs and a window incorporating stained glass from Winckley Square.

One of the proudest possessions brought from the old Club was a picture, *The Defence of Rorke's Drift*, which recorded the heroic stand of a small body of British

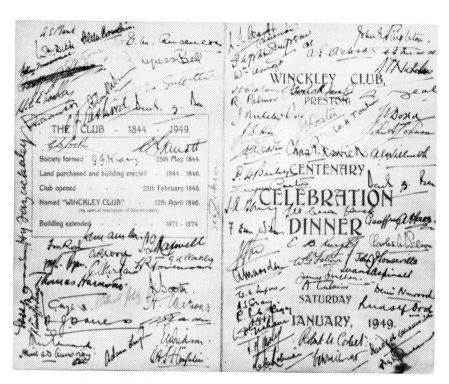

Back of the Celebration Dinner menu bearing signatures

MENU

COCKTAILS

SHERRY
Amontillado
HOCK
Niersteiner 1943/1945
CLARET
Château Langoa
Barton 1934
Château Angludet 1934
BURGUNDY
Moulin à Vent 1933
Pommard
CHAMPAGNE
Clicquot 1934
PORT
Warre 1922
BRANDY
Rouyer Guillet
BENEDICTINE D.O.M.
BOLSKUMMEL

HORS D'OEUVRES

Turtle Soup
*
Fillets of
Sole Bonne Femme
*
Lamb Cutlets
*
Sorbet
*
Roast Turkey
*
Pêche Melba
*
Cheese Savoury
*
Dessert
*
Coffee
*

The Defence of Rorke's Drift *by Alphonse de Neuville*

soldiers at the pass of Rorke's Drift in Natal in 1879. On that occasion, two young lieutenants called Chard and Bromhead with about eighty men repulsed an army of some 4,000 Zulus. They had to build make-shift defences very hurriedly, which were mainly of mealie bags and biscuit tins; defences which the Zulus penetrated six times, but on each occasion were driven back by bayonets. The Zulus suffered heavy losses and withdrew after a battle of almost eleven hours. Mercifully, the post was relieved soon afterwards by the main British forces. No less than eleven Victoria Crosses were awarded for this gallant action.

Years later, in 1890, Lt Col Chard who had been the senior officer at Rorke's Drift and, with Lt Bromhead, had headed the list of those awarded the Victoria Cross, came to live at Sumners Hotel in Fulwood, Preston. He remained there for six years and, along with the Rev G. Smith who had been the Chaplain at Rorke's Drift and also lived at Sumners Hotel, became a member of the Winckley Club. No wonder that the Club prized the famous picture in which Lt Chard, as he was at the time of the battle, can be seen bare-headed on the right, holding a rifle, and Chaplain Smith, in a dark coat, handing out ammunition. The original of this picture is in the National Army Museum.

Sadly, the new Winckley Club in Garstang Road did not prosper, and the premises were sold to British Telecom, however, the Club did not close down but found a new home in the Officers' Mess of Kimberley Barracks, (Fulwood) where it remained until the troubles in Northern Ireland made it impossible for civilians to use army premises. An unfortunate occurrence during the Club's stay there was the disappearance of the

Lt John Rouse Merriott Chard VC*

Rev George Smith

cherished picture of *The Defence of Rorke's Drift*, which had been signed by Lt Col Chard and Chaplain Smith.

Now the Winckley Club meets monthly for eight months of the year at Preston Golf Club in Fulwood. The members still have many treasured possessions from the old Club in Winckley Square and retain many of the old traditions. The lady subscribers participate fully in all these activities and also enjoy a flourishing section of their own.

*He later served in many posts in England, finally retiring and staying in the Sumners Hotel in Preston, where he died on 26/27th November 1918 from bronchial trouble which had afflicted him for six months. After a small military ceremony, he was buried in the Church of England plot in New Hall Lane cemetery in Preston.

The Literary and Philosophical Institution, Preston

The Literary and Philosophical Institution

The Literary and Philosophical Institution, designed by local architect, Mr John Welch, was built at the same time as the Winckley Club which it adjoined. It was formally opened on 9th December 1846 and contained a Newsroom, Billiard and Chess Rooms, Collegiate Hall, Library and Museum. At first it flourished considerably; many important lectures, always well-attended, were given there. But, sadly, its fortunes declined and, in 1868, the building with its contents was sold to the Corporation of Preston and became known as Dr Shepherd's Library and Museum. It housed the wonderful collection of books which had been left to the town in 1761 by Dr Richard Shepherd. In 1895 this was transferred to the Reference Library at the Harris Museum where it remains to the present day.

The Grammar School

The Grammar School was erected in Cross Street in 1841, because the locality of the earlier school, Stoneygate, had declined in respectability to become 'one of the very lowest parts of the town'. The architect was again Mr John Welch and funds for its construction were provided by private shareholders. It was not until February 1860 that Preston Corporation bought the Grammar School for £1,527 10s.

The Grammar School

THE PEEL STATUE

The Peel statue, on the eastern side of the Square, facing Cross Street, was erected by public subscription in 1852, being carved out of a single block of limestone by local sculptor, Mr Thomas Duckett.

Preston had a great deal of respect for Robert Peel, who sacrificed his political career to repeal the hated Corn Laws, and the many processions which passed through the Square often paused here.

The 7ft 6ins plot of land on which it stands was conveyed in an indenture, made 31st May 1852, to the mayor, aldermen and burgesses of Preston by James German of Whittingham House Esq, for a 'consideration' of £21. The statue was ceremoniously unveiled the same day, Whit Monday 1852, by the Mayor, Alderman T. Monk and a distinguished company of gentlemen. It is inscribed:

SIR

ROBERT PEEL

BARONET

Erected by Public Subscription, 1852.

The Peel statue

NO. 7 WINCKLEY SQUARE

Every day hundreds of people pass these premises without noticing on the wall to the left of the entrance a stone plaque:

It marks the spot where the ashes of James Todd, a wealthy Preston accountant, are interred in the wall of his old office. These offices are now occupied by Messrs Garratt, Son & Flowerdew Limited, insurance brokers [now Napthens Solicitors], and a covenant, dated 1954, which is now in the possession of the head of the firm, Mr John Garratt, states that the remains must not be removed and the stone must be kept in a good state.

Mr Todd died at the age of 68 after a seizure while attending Haydock Park racecourse, of which he was a director. He had trained in Preston as an accountant and opened his own office two years after qualifying. He rapidly built up an extensive practice and dealt with many enterprises throughout Britain and the world. As well as Preston he had offices in London, Manchester, Blackpool and Chester. Before the Russian Revolution these even extended to Moscow where his firm were accountants to an iron and steel company.

He was also chairman of Sunbeam Motors which later became part of the vast Darracq concern which had works in Britain and France. During World War I he was engaged in supplying munitions and aircraft engines to the British, French and Italian governments.

Mr Todd's home was Farington Lodge, near Leyland, from which he was brought to the office in a magnificent, chauffeur-driven Sunbeam motor car. The late Mr Walter Hunniball, who trained as an accountant in his office, recalled in a newspaper interview that 'When in Preston, Mr Todd's day at the office began with being shaved by his barber, Mr Coward, whose shop was in Lune Street.'

In the Harris Museum and Art Gallery there is a beautiful painting, completed in 1920 by William Logsdail, which shows Mr Todd's three daughters in the drawing room of Farington Lodge. After her husband's death, Mrs Todd sold the house to Leyland Motors for use as a guest house for distinguished overseas clients.

Mr Todd's firm still continues, having its Preston office in nearby Starkie Street, and branches in other towns [now one office in Adelphi Street, Preston].

THE RESIDENCE OF WILLIAM AINSWORTH

At the southern corner of Cross Street stood another very beautiful building, the Italian-style villa of William Ainsworth, cotton manufacturer, whose RULES TO BE OBEYED BY THE OPERATIVES in his mill in Cotton Court were nothing short of slavery. They bore evidence of long working hours, restrictions on personal freedom, and a ruthless system of fines which the management did not fail to enforce in the courts.

Italian-style villa, Winckley Square. The residence of William Ainsworth 1862, photograph by Robert Pateson

After the death of William Ainsworth in 1862, the villa was acquired by Mr Parker, a wealthy grocer. It then became known as 'Pepper Hall', possibly because its owner was known as 'Pepper' Parker!

Dr Hammond, who followed Mr Parker, was the last private resident before the villa passed into commercial hands. In the 1940s it was a County Court Office, named 'Winckley House' and was still regarded as a beautiful building whose demolition in favour of a modern construction bearing the same name was much regretted.

Mr Ainsworth's villa was numbered 11 Winckley Square. The house next door, no. 12, was once the home of John Humber, cotton manufacturer, but about 1910, when it became the headquarters of the Royal Lancashire Agricultural Society, it was known as Derby House, because Lord Derby was the President of that Society. This house marks the end of the eastern side of Winckley Square; beyond it lies Starkie Street. For nos. 13 to 19 one must cross to the southern side, and for nos. 20 to 34 to the western side. Beyond no. 34, formerly the entrance to the Catholic College, lies Chapel Street.

Winckley Square, south side, 1863, photograph by Robert Pateson

THE WESTERN SIDE OF WINCKLEY SQUARE

The western side of Winckley Square was to become almost entirely devoted to the education of Catholic boys and girls. In 1865, to rival the Grammar School in Cross Street, a Catholic Grammar School was opened in rented accommodation at no. 25 Winckley Square.

Further along the western side of the Square, between nos. 34 and 35, was a narrow passage which gave access to a short row of cottages called Mount Pleasant. One of these was purchased and, in 1866, the Catholic Grammar School transferred there. In due course, all the cottages in Mount Pleasant were purchased, together with some in Mount Street and Lythgoe Place.

Winckley Square, west side, 1863, photograph by Robert Pateson

In 1875 the school had grown considerably and it was again transferred; this time to no. 29 Winckley Square, formerly the home of cotton manufacturer, Mr George Paley. There it remained until 1897 when reorganisation brought sweeping changes.

In January 1898, work on new college buildings began and the school was temporarily homeless. Preston Corporation, therefore, allowed it to use Dr Shepherd's Library at the corner of Cross Street, next to the rival Protestant Grammar School. The new building which emerged was named the Catholic College, alma mater to many Prestonians.

With the reorganisation of Catholic education in Preston in 1978 this has now been absorbed into Newman College and has recently left the Square for new accommodation at Lark Hill.

The main entrance of the Catholic College, Preston

The photograph [in the first edition] by M. P. McCann, with diagrams of the site of the College buildings in 1865 and 1970 and the accompanying text are extracted from *A Centenary History of the Catholic College, Preston* and reproduced here by kind permission of the author, Mr Alban Hindle BA (Ref. P373.42721 Harris Reference Library).

For the education of Catholic girls, the Convent of the Holy Child Jesus opened in Winckley Square in 1875, when the nuns bought no. 23, formerly the home of

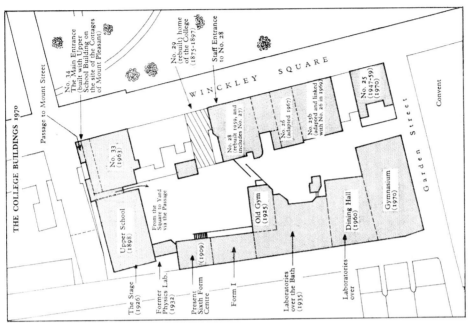

THE COLLEGE BUILDINGS 1970

Passage to Mount Street

No. 34
The Main Entrance
(built with Upper
School Building on
the site of the Cottages
of Mount Pleasant)

No. 29
(rebuilt) home
of the College
(1875-1897)

Staff Entrance
to No. 28

WINCKLEY SQUARE

No. 33
(1963)

No. 28
(rebuilt 1959, and
includes No. 27)

No. 26
(adapted 1967)

No. 25b
(adapted and linked
with No. 26 in 1969)

No. 25
(1947-59)
(1970)

Upper School
(1898)

From the
Square to Yard
via the Passage

Gymnasium
(1970)

Garden Street

Convent

The Stage
(1926)

Former
Physics Lab.
(1932)

Present
Sixth Form
Centre
(1909)

Form I

Old Gym
(1925)

Laboratories
over the Bath
(1935)

Dining Hall
(1960)

Laboratories
over

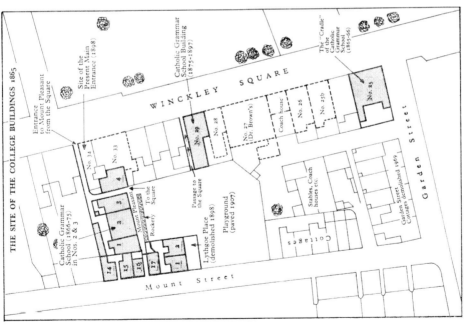

THE SITE OF THE COLLEGE BUILDINGS 1865

Entrance
to Mount Pleasant
from the Square

Site of the
Present Main
Entrance (1898)

Catholic Grammar
School Building
(1875-1897)

The "Cradle"
of the
Catholic
Grammar
School
(1865-66)

WINCKLEY SQUARE

No. 34

No. 33

No. 29

No. 28

No. 27
(Dr. Brown's)

Coach house

No. 26

No. 25b

No. 25

Catholic Grammar
School (1865-75)
in Nos. 2 & 3

Mount Pleasant

To the
Rockery

To the
Square

Passage to
the Square

Playground
(paved 1907)

Lythgoe Place
(demolished 1898)

Stables, Coach
houses etc.

Cottages

Garden Street
Cottages demolished 1969

Garden Street

Mount Street

The site of the College buildings 1865 and 1970

THE STORY OF WINCKLEY SQUARE, PRESTON   57

Thomas Batty Addison, the Recorder of Preston, for £2,000. They also rented no. 22 until, in 1878, they were able to buy it for the exorbitant sum, so it seemed to them, of £3,000!

The school prospered and the nuns acquired other property in Winckley Square, Ribblesdale Place and Garden Street. In 1935, a new chapel was opened, the old one becoming the domestic science room. Still more property was acquired in 1944, in Ribblesdale Place and East Cliff but with the re-organisation of secondary education in 1978, Winckley Square Convent was absorbed into Newman College. Three years later, in 1981, it was closed and put up for sale.

These facts and the sketch reproduced below are extracted from a [Centenary] pamphlet Ref. P373 in the Harris Reference Library, entitled *Winckley Square Convent School 1875–1975*, and reproduced by kind permission.

Drawing of Winckley Square Convent

'Drawings and plans of Winckley Square a hundred years ago certainly give a very pleasing picture. The exterior of the houses has changed but little, and in the old prints we can recognise our own doors and windows; Garden Street still deserved its name, and "at the back of number 22 was a long sunny garden – beyond it fields, with trees and hawthorn hedges. The railway was as then a small affair and seemed a long way off".'

THE PRESTON AND COUNTY CATHOLIC CLUB

The Preston and County Catholic Club was founded in 1906 at the instigation of Father Canning SJ, who was on the staff of St Wilfrid's Church in Preston. A letter of proposal which was subsequently issued bore the names of prominent Catholic gentlemen who had been present at the inaugural meeting on Wednesday 30th May:

Major Anderton	A. Mooney Esq	T. L. Smith Esq
C. Eastwood Esq	H. C. Pilkington Esq	S. Wilkinson Esq
R. Hull Esq	C. J. Pyke Esq	W. Wood Esq

The main object of the Club was to provide a headquarters for the promotion of Catholic interests.

Although there were already two well-established Catholic bodies in the neighbourhood, the First Catholic Charitable Society, and the Broughton Charitable Society, they only met infrequently, and it was felt that in view of the many serious problems which faced the Catholics at this time, not least among them being education, Catholic interests would benefit from a permanent centre of action.

The Club, essentially non-political in character, aimed to bring together Catholic professional and business gentlemen from all over Lancashire; hence the title, The Preston and County Catholic Club. A limited company was formed bearing that name, with its registered office at no. 4 Winckley Square, the house on the south-western corner of Winckley Street, formerly owned by Nicholas Grimshaw. Here the Club opened, duly fitted up with 'all the up-to-date requirements of a Social Club, i.e. Reading Rooms, supplied with leading periodicals, Catholic and Non-Catholic; a Reference Library, especially consisting of standard Catholic works on topics of public interest; Refreshment Rooms, Billiards, etc., etc.'

Until the 1960s the Club occupied the whole of no. 4 Winckley Square, after which the ground floor was let off for office accommodation and the Club confined its operation to the upper floors only. In 1973 it moved to the western side of Winckley Square, to no. 30 where, because of the proximity of the Catholic College, it became closely connected with the Preston Catholic College Association.

Finally, on 31st July 1988, the Preston and County Catholic Club moved out of Winckley Square to hospitable quarters in Columba House, Deepdale Road, Preston, where it thrives anew [regrettably the Club closed in the early 1990s].

CONCLUSION

Winckley Square has always been admired. Thus Hardwick in 1857 wrote that 'In point of extent and picturesque beauty, this provincial *rus in urbe* might successfully compete with many in the metropolis.'

Pollard in 1882 stated, 'It has for many years past been deservedly regarded as one of the most ornamental and picturesque squares of which any town can boast. It has long been the residence of several of the most wealthy families in the town, and its beautifully laid out central gardens, with their profusion of trees in full and ample foliage, impart to it a suburban rather than an urban character, even in the midst of town-life surroundings.'

But on 9th of March 1933, the *Lancashire Evening Post* commented, 'Winckley Square, like most of its London prototypes, is no longer an exclusive residential centre for wealthy and fashionable citizens. Most of the dwellings are occupied as offices by lawyers, accountants, land, estate and insurance agencies, and as chambers of companies of many varieties. A few still remain as residences of professional men, Clubs, High Schools, and one or two hotels may be found there.'[1]

'. . . but not yet have any shops invaded its seclusion. The central gardens are still as quiet and secluded a bird sanctuary as ever, though no longer as carefully attended. There are so many busy folk among the tenants who have no time for garden tending, no leisure for garden lounging . . .'

'In spite of the modern invasion of motors and the use of half the roads in the Square as a car park, Winckley Square is not yet quite a common thoroughfare, and still retains much of its dignity and quietness.'

On 21st July 1950, a very sad article appeared in the *Preston Herald*, written by historian Mr J. H. Spencer. It was entitled 'The Decline and Fall of Winckley Square' and is quoted here in its entirety:

'We live in an impatient and revolutionary age and whenever I pass through Winckley Square I invariably stand for a few moments and survey it from the north side. Here you are on the top of a slight incline and from this vantage point can judge its restful beauty and its old-world charm. For it is an oasis of temporary relaxation from the adjacent busy streets of our modern world.

From the present condition of this square one might think that we are so much concerned with the grandiose town planning schemes of the future that we have forgotten this beauty spot on our own doorstep, inherited from a previous generation. Its appearance today is one of pitiful neglect; it dumbly appeals to you and will do so more insistently as time passes.

In these summer days it resembles a jungle of wild over-grown weeds, unrestrained, untrimmed bushes, and a miniature forest of towering trees with here and there a few rhododendron blooms bravely asserting themselves'.

[1] I know of only one hotel, Worth's Commercial Hotel, at no. 25 Winckley Square, at the corner of Garden Street.

A century ago

In contrast to its present state, it is refreshing to look at two views of it found in Hardwick's *History of Preston*, dated 1857. These give some indication of its appearance nearly one hundred years ago. It was then a typical London square and conveys the impression of a neat and elegant private park in which the residents delighted to promenade. In fact, some of these promenaders are shown on the two views, ladies dressed in the fashion of the period, wearing bonnets and swinging crinoline dresses, escorted by top-hatted, frock-coated gentlemen. Seats are also discernible for their convenience.

Winckley Square a century ago was essentially the residential centre of the gentry of Preston and many of its houses bear evidence of having been homes of spacious luxury. Some of them, such as the Miller mansion, now the Junior Park School, [Blackthorn Homes] would require several servants, and most would have at least one or two domestics to keep them in decent condition.

The days of the Victorian white-capped servitude are gone never to return, still, these old Georgian and early nineteenth-century houses have a fascination for me. They vary in design and construction, there is no standard uniformity about them and the materials and craftsmanship are so enduring that even now in decline they look fine and seasoned. They belong to a world that worried about social distinctions and thought so little about the living conditions of the unfortunate poor. Today, education, commerce and bureaucracy have succeeded their former occupants. The trek to the suburbs began with the turn into the present century and has been completed with the advent of the motor car.

After their departure, the square deteriorated and since it was not anyone's business to care for the amenities of the gardens, they have become, not a joy for ever but an eyesore and a reproof to our aesthetic susceptibilities.

Tradition and the humanities are now forgotten in this square; it is given over to youthful education, professional, commercial and governmental activities. Centuries of great men who have gone before them do not ruffle the imagination of the present occupants, otherwise they would not have neglected some slight token of commemoration for July 2nd, the centenary of the death of Sir Robert Peel, whose statue graces the square. The great statesman who 'gave us cheaper bread', should surely be remembered by the descendants of those who, in 1852, subscribed £622 for this statue to perpetuate his many virtues. Some little floral tribute, say a wreath of red roses at the feet of the great reformer, would have stirred the curiosity of passing pedestrians.

I passed it a few days ago; it is the only thing of beauty here which can now give pleasure to the beholder. Bravely it stands on its high pediment, strenuously defying time, wild nature and above all the nearby encircling trees in their endeavour to destroy it.

Keep its character

Let us hope that our civic authorities will tackle this square boldly and courageously by cleaning up and destroying the weed undergrowth of years, designing and replanning the greenswards and flower beds, doing away with many of the huge trees which block the beautiful vistas of the surroundings.

On no account should any part of it be devoted to games; it should be retained as far as possible in keeping with its original layout and it will then be an actual example of an early Victorian town square in all its loveliness, mellowed and enriched by local tradition and human associations.

Philosophical Institution and residence of William Ainsworth.
One of the two views in Hardwick's History of Preston, *1857 mentioned by Mr Spencer*

Our civic authorities did 'tackle this square boldly and courageously'. In 1951 a number of agreements were signed between the landowners and Preston Borough Council which effectively placed the responsibility for the maintenance of the land-scaped area in the hands of the local authority. During the Second World War this area had reached its full decline when a water tank for civil defence purposes and air raid shelters appeared amid the trees. Even the railings were removed to help the the war effort. Eventually Winckley Square was declared a public open space and the Parks Department turned it from a tangle of undergrowth and decaying trees into a very pleasant old corner: a reminder of the town's antiquity.

In 1957, however, Preston's growing traffic problem caused eyes to turn to the square as a convenient means of taking vehicles from the main streets. It was packed

Winckley Square from the south.
One of the two views in Hardwick's History of Preston, *1857 mentioned by Mr Spencer*

solidly, every day, with businessmen's cars; herring-bone parking was suggested, and there was the awful theory, supported by the Mayor, of all people, that the contour of the grassed area would lend itself to a two-floor car park at the upper end and gardens at the lower end!

So much feeling was generated by these proposals that, happily for us, they came to nought. Indeed, in 1985, our civic authorities again took action to restore the square to its former glory. Many shrubs were planted, some mature trees, found to be dead, were chopped down and replaced by young ones; others were drastically pruned to improve the vistas. The railings were at last replaced and the setting of the Peel statue improved.

Winckley Square is now designated a conservation area, all buildings therein being subjected to the requirements of such an area. I think William Cross would have approved of such action. His central area does indeed 'lie forever open and unbuilt upon' and the civic authorities are now taking as much trouble as he and his wife Ellen took to preserve the special quality of Winckley Square, for which we are truly thankful!

WINCKLEY SQUARE IN 2008

Aidan Turner-Bishop

Marian Roberts wrote *The Story of Winckley Square, Preston* in 1988 and, in the intervening twenty years, the Square has naturally changed, and further changes are planned. A walk round Winckley Square in September 2008 shows what has changed.

1 Chapel Street / 1 Winckley Place is no longer occupied by the Britannic Assurance, who once painted the windows and drainpipes in a bright blue, but by Smith Winston & Co, solicitors. St Wilfrid's Presbytery is unchanged. Inghams Solicitors occupy the Grimshaw residence at the corner of Winckley Street, which has been repaved with setts and fitted with uncomfortable-looking stone benches. Traffic still uses Winckley Street – albeit one-way – so the attempt to create a relaxed, café side-street has not worked.

Thomas Miller's house at 5 Winckley Square was sold by Preston College, which succeded Tuson College, and was converted into apartments by Blackthorn developers. An underground car park, accessed from Winckley Street, has been constructed beneath the house. A plaque, installed by Preston & South Ribble Civic Trust, records that Thomas Miller (1811–1865) built the house in 1845, aged 34, and that he donated land for Miller Park in 1864, a year before his death, age 54. dwf Solicitors have taken over no. 6 from the Norwich Union. Napthens Solicitors still occupy no. 7 where James Todd's ashes are sealed in the wall. Various firms use 9 and 10 as offices; HM Revenue & Customs are still in no. 8.

Winckley House, the austere brick offices of Lancashire County Council, still stands although the door to Winckley Square is usually closed and its porch looks shabby and dilapidated. Offices at no. 12, Derby House, have been recently re-let. Robert House, 2 Starkie Street, is now the Bizz Kidz nursery: a sign of the times when both parents work, supporting large home mortgages.

Rushtons, accountants, occupy the corner of Starkie Street and Winckley Square. Their offices are normally brightly flood-lit at night, attracting many insects in summer. Tucked in the courtyard at 13A is another contemporary business: Winckley Square Clinic which offers cosmetic treatments such as Botox injections, laser (IPL) depilation and glycolic face peels. Like many other business in Winckley Square, the clinic has an internet website: www.winckleysquareclinic.co.uk. A website celebrating Winckley Square www.winckleysquare.org.uk was created in the late 1990s; Marian Roberts contributed to its compilation and replied to enquiries submitted to the site.

Charnley House at no. 13, with its yellow door, houses Thurnhills Solicitors. Hedley & Co., stockbrokers, occupy premises in the side court. Nos. 14 and 15 appear to be changing hands: surveyors Bailey Deakin Hamilton used 14; the Lancashire Care NHS Foundation Trust was in no. 15 and 5 Camden Place. Barristers work from no. 16, St John's Buildings. No. 17 has reverted to a family home, housing the architect Dominic Roberts, the author Sally Stone and their family. Like new apartments elsewhere, this represents a return to inner-city living on the Square, a notable change since 1988. Francis Roberts Architects' office is in the Studio at no. 17. The practice is well-known for the restoration of St John's Minster and St Walburge's church, Preston, and the design of the RIBA Award-winning Lantern House arts centre in Ulverston. Next door, no. 18, is the Children & Family Court Advisory and Support Service. No. 19 seems to be a private home.

Across the road, the Holy Child Jesus Convent and School (1875–1978) is now apartments. In 2005 Paul Heathcote, the Longridge-based restaurateur, divided his Simply Heathcotes restaurant, opened in 1995, into the Chop House, on the ground floor, and the Olive Press bistro, in the basement. Looking down Garden Street, towards the Fishergate Centre car park and along the line of the Syke river, one can see the former Newman College Sports Hall, built in 1970, which is planned to be redeveloped by Trovit Homes as 47 new apartments. No. 1 Garden Street houses solicitors and a call centre.

Premises on the west side of Winckley Square – nos. 25 to 35 – are occupied by a variety of service sector companies. There seems to be a busy turnover of firms on this side; in September 2008 there were eight advertised properties for sale or let. Perhaps some of these may return to residential use? Companies in this stretch include Fine & Country Residential Sales (25); recruitment agencies; A I Cherry, auditors and 'forensic accounting' (26); Howarth Goodman solicitors (25B). Edith Rigby's house, at no. 28, appears to be unoccupied. The National Centre for Restorative Justice is based in no. 30, Winckley Chambers. Rational House, at no. 32, no longer houses a friendly society; it is now used by ITN Mark Education who recruit supply teachers.

The former Preston Catholic College (1865–1978) is now the oddly-named iQor House which sells 'recovery services' and 'retention management'. iQor is an American-based multi-national company which specialises in call centre management and services like debt recovery. No. 35, at the Square's corner with Chapel Street, looks mainly unoccupied but may house the ITV Pensions Department.

Some of the Square's street furniture has changed. Parking meter machines, looking in profile like portly policemen, have appeared. Some are powered by solar panels. On both sides of the Square, Royal Mail has installed rectangular, cast-iron, type G pillar boxes. This design, dating from 1974, was based on an original design by David Mellor, the cutlery designer.

The centre of the Square was the subject of a design competition in early 2008. The plans, which include a 64-jet water fountain, fibre optic lighting and pink and grey granite laid in a woven pattern, were designed by Cooper Partnership, a Bristol-based practice. It is also planned to fell a quarter of the trees in the Square and to suspend metal letters of the alphabet – spelling 'Winckley Square' [14 in all] – from some of the remaining trees; letters will also be attached to railings and set in the grass. The historical interpretation board, next to Peel's statue, is to be removed as it 'clutters' the design. Quite what Marian Roberts would have made of these plans we can only guess.

SUBSCRIBERS

Tom Abbot
Mrs Miriam Aldred
His Honour Herbert Andrew
    and Netty Andrew
Dean Archer
Florence and William Archer
Thomas J. Arkwright

Mrs J. C. Bailey
Avis Balmer
Mr and Mrs F. J. Baron
Mr H. B. Barton
Ms L. M. Barton
Tim Beals
Mark Belderbos
Peter Benson
Mr and Mrs R. Berry
Jean Bickerstaff
David and Paula Bloomer
Irene Mary Bolton
Beryl Bowcott
Steven John Bradley
Catherine Bretherton
John and Janice Bretherton
Mike and Elsa Bridges
Michael Briggs
Hilary Brown
Michael and Judith Brown
Phyllis Brown
Christine Burns

Terry Casey
Robert Brindle Catterall
Sam and Lisa Chapman
R. Cizdyn
Julia Clark
Diana and Terry Clarke
Marilyn Cliff
John B. Coogan
C. J. Cooper
Canon D. Cooper

Martin Cooper
Ian John Crabtree
Mr A. N. Craven
Philip and Jo Craven
Adrian Russell Crook
Anthony Assheton Cross
Mrs Stella M. Cunliffe

Jim Danby
Roy D'Eye
Ann Dewhurst
Margaret B. Dickinson
Diana Dioszeghy
Kendal Downs
Tim Downs
Mona Duggan
Barbara Dyer

Mrs Muriel J. Eastham
Marjorie and Derek Edwards
William Eves and Patricia Eves

Elizabeth Fearnley
Rob Feeley
William M. Fetherstone
A. A. Fisher
Steve Fishwick
T. Flaherty
Audrey Flannery
Tony and Ann Fletcher
Rosemary Forrest
Brenda M. Fox
Francis Roberts Architects
J. Fullerton
Michael and Elisabeth Furness

Stephen and Susan Gardner
Mrs J. M. Gartland
Mr John William Gerald
Janet and Richard Gibb
Angela and James Glithero

SUBSCRIBERS

Stephen Gregson
Mrs B. F. Gunn

Dennys Haigh
M. Hall
Michael H. Halewood
Stephen R. Halliwell
Howard Hammersley
Teresa Harrison
Dave and Gloria Harris
Joe Harris
Christopher Harrison
Michael Harrison
Mrs Janet Healy, San Mateo,
  California USA
Ann Heath, Florida USA
Liz Hedley
Andrew Hobbs
Joe Hodgson
David Hodgkinson
Jennifer Holt
Pat Holt
Julia Horn
Leslie Howarth
Sandra E. Hudson
Frank and Linda Hughes

Linda and David Ianson

Anne and Charles Francis Jackson
Mrs Joyce James
Peter Jelley
Teresa Johnson
Mrs Rosemary Jolly
Alan Jones MRCIS

Anne-Marie Kelly (neé Feeley)
P. Kelly
David Kerry
T. H. Kirkham MD FRCS
Wendy Klinkenberg

Ron Knight
Janice Knights
Andrew and Victoria Kok
Greta Krypczyk-Oddy
Geoffrey Law
Zoë Lawson
Mrs D. A. Lester
Barry and Margaret Lewis
F. M. Longmaid
Carol Lowde
Mr Christian Lowde

Hilary Machell
Paul Martin
Janet Martindale
Alan Mason
Nicola Mather
Patricia Maudsley
T. McClelland
Cath McDiarmid
Mrs B. S. McDonald
Eileen McKavanagh
Hilda McLaughlin
Bernard and Janet Melling
Mrs R. Melling
Wilf Melling
Mrs Joan Metcalfe
J. E. Moffat
Arnold A. Monk
Mrs M Moon
Alice I. Murray and Jack J. Murray

Mr and Mrs Mark Naylor
Mr Kim Nicholson
Teresa Nicklin
Anne Nixon

Dorothy Painter
Peter Park
Anne Parkinson
Barbara Parkinson

SUBSCRIBERS

Michael and Penelope Pattinson
Mrs Elizabeth Pearson
  and Mr Mike Pearson
Margaret and Tony Pettit
David and June Phillips
Pauline Phillips
Eric Prescott
Barbara Alice Proctor
M. Purdy

Nellie Race
Mrs Enid Rainford
Mr David K. Rhodes
Brett and Martha Richardson
Barbara A. Richmond
Dominic Roberts and Sally Stone
Jean Robinson
Margaret Robinson

St Wilfrid's RC Church
Rosie Samad
Terence P. Sargeant
Christine Seddon
Elizabeth Shorrock
The Lord Shuttleworth
Roy Shuttleworth
John Siddall
Nigel and Kay Sladen
Dr Frank Slater
Betty Smith
Mark Smith
Tom Smith
Mrs Mary Sontag
Ann Spoors
Donald Mackay Stables

Kathleen Starkie
John Stokes
Lyn Stokes
Peter Sullivan
Michael Swift

Mrs B. J. Taylor
Nigel Taylor
The Talbot Library
Geoffrey J. Thompson
Mrs J. F. Thompson
Jane Thorpe
Miss Helen Tomlinson
Andrea and Philip Treacy
John and Mary Turner
Leslie Turner
Mike and Sue Turner

Tony and Jill Wadeson
David and Christine Walmsley
Dorothy Walmsley
Mrs Cynthia Warbrick
John J. Ward
Timothy F. Ward
Susan Warlow
Gwen Weiss
Peter and Andrée Whalley
William Whiteside
Catherine Wignall
Muriel Wilson
Mr D. Williams
Flo Wood
T. Woodcock
J. A. Woods
Patricia Ann and Alan Winston Woods